★NICK FITZH

PRESENTATION
MAGIC!

ACHIEVING OUTSTANDING BUSINESS
PRESENTATIONS USING THE RULES OF MAGIC

Marshall Cavendish
Business

Cover design: Opal Works Co. Limited

Published in 2011 by Marshall Cavendish Business
An imprint of Marshall Cavendish International

PO Box 65829, London EC1P 1NY, United Kingdom
info@marshallcavendish.co.uk

and

1 New Industrial Road, Singapore 536196
genrefsales@sg.marshallcavendish.com
www.marshallcavendish.com/genref

Other Marshall Cavendish offices:
Marshall Cavendish Corporation. 99 White Plains Road, Tarrytown NY 10591-9001,
USA • Marshall Cavendish International (Thailand) Co Ltd. 253 Asoke, 12th Flr,
Sukhumvit 21 Road, Klongtoey Nua, Wattana, Bangkok 10110, Thailand • Marshall
Cavendish (Malaysia) Sdn Bhd. Times Subang, Lot 46, Subang Hi-Tech Industrial Park,
Batu Tiga, 40000 Shah Alam, Selangor Darul Ehsan, Malaysia

Marshall Cavendish is a trademark of Times Publishing Limited

A CIP record for this book is available from the British Library

ISBN 978-981-4328-31-9

Printed and bound in Great Britain by
TJ International Limited, Padstow, Cornwall

*I dedicate this book to all the magicians around the world
who have been good enough to share their creativity,
learned advice and inspiration.*

*Reinventing everything I do career-wise has given me
a whole new lease of life. For that I am also indebted to
The Magic Circle and to Paula, Louis and Eliza
for loving support on the home front.*

CONTENTS

THE RULES of MAGIC

applied to
BUSINESS COMMUNICATION

Engagement	Attention

Engagement

1 The framework for any communication is determined by the **expectations and perceptions that you trigger**

2 Expectations and perceptions can be reinforced or diminished by **Prestige, Atmosphere & Environment and Desire**

3 Communication can only register effectively when it builds on **what the audience already knows**

4 The **brain filters** out most information it receives, leaving only what it considers important

Attention

5 Concentrated attention requires a single point of focus

6 Attention tracks from left to right, then settles at the left

7 The audience will look where you look, where you point, where you tell them to look

8 Curiosity, movement, sound, contrast and anything that is new or different are friends and foes. Each has the potential to seize attention.

9 The wider environment can often add to or detract from your message

10 Every element of your content will either add to or detract from your message

11 Attention is sustained by variation, which shortens mental time

Impact

12 The senses offer **five different ways** into the brain

13 Firsts and lasts are remembered

14 Negatives impede communication as they need unscrambling before the meaning can be interpreted

15 Over-familiarity leads to 'invisibility'

16 Sustained impact depends on transferring information **to long-term memory**

Conviction

17 To be convincing you, yourself, must **be convinced**

18 Doubts are reduced by **openness**, but may be increased by **over-stressing**

19 People put more reliance on something they have **worked out for themselves**

20 People's reactions are influenced by those of their **peers**

INTRODUCTION

Ask most magicians what got them started and they will invariably tell you tales that begin with receiving a first magic set at around the age of six. For me it was very different; it started in 1991 when I was running a PR company and needed some entertainment for my staff party. I hired a magician called Fay Presto whose talents included pushing lit cigarettes through guests' jackets and bottles through solid tables, while your own bank notes floated in mid-air. Fay did all this and much more besides, and from that moment I was hooked – I sought out the shops, the clubs, the magazines and the conventions. Magic also started creeping into new business pitches for my PR company and this got me mingling with magical inventors and some extraordinary thinkers.

The more I learned about magic, the more I started to think that many of the principles that lay behind the tricks could be extremely useful in business. Directing attention, persuading and convincing were, after all, what my job as a PR consultant was all about. If you leave aside the deception elements, it seemed to me that the world's magicians and I were essentially in the same game. Confirmation came from James Randi, who as the Great Randi is widely admired as one of the gurus of the magic world. He said: "Magicians are the world's greatest communicators; it's just that everything they are telling you is wrong!"

So there really was scope, I thought, to apply the psychological principles that lay behind the tricks to something more useful than simply pulling rabbits out of hats and making perfectly useful items disappear. My early immersion into magic happily coincided with the emergence of a new breed of young magicians, such as Andy

Nyman, Marc Paul and Anthony Owen, who were performing at John Lenahan's Monday Night Magic club nights in London pubs. They had a fresh take on magic that leant towards mind reading and deployed a range of associated psychological skills. Eventually another magician appeared from the restaurant scene in Bristol. His name was Derren Brown, and when I saw his first lecture at a magic convention in the late '90s, everybody's jaws dropped to the floor. He soon teamed up with Owen and Nyman to make TV programmes, and the rest is history. Importantly for me, Derren's arrival brought fresh new reference points to the world of magic – no longer would people's perceptions of magic be confined to memories of childhood parties and the likes of Paul Daniels and Tommy Cooper.

Eventually I plucked up the courage to apply for membership of The Magic Circle – the world's foremost magic society with a massive library and access to many of the world's greatest magical minds. These resources enabled me to refine my thinking and identify the Rules of Magic – 20 principles that are used instinctively by the best magicians, and that I believe prove equally effective in business. The Rules are really quite simple; that, for me, is where their beauty lies, and it is the magical context that brings them alive.

The Rules are very much about *why* magic works rather than how it works. I am not allowed to tell anyone how magic works – I would be expelled from The Magic Circle in fairly short order! What I probably can risk revealing is that one of the reasons it is so important to keep the secrets is that many are so childishly simple you would be severely disappointed were you to uncover them. More often than not it really is almost all in the presentation.

When I first meet the people I am coaching in Presentation Skills with The Rules of Magic, I explain that coming up is everything they would expect from more standard training programmes, with the addition of principles I have gleaned from the world of magic.

I usually start with a short introduction to the principles, along the following lines:

> I take out a pack of cards and shuffle them, as I tell everyone I am a member of the world famous Magic Circle. I say that we meet at a very secret place on Monday nights, before revealing that it's actually near London's Euston Station and if they ever need a lovely venue for a corporate event it makes a fine choice. Some people know it and we have a brief chat about the HQ to build some rapport. On Monday nights, however, it is full of magicians of all shapes and sizes, many huddled around tables showing each other card tricks. As I continue to shuffle my cards I paint a scenario of myself among the magicians. "Pick a card," I say, "any card. Where would you like me to stop?" They indicate a choice and I ask if they would like to change their mind. Eventually they pick a card, show it to the others and I start to supposedly read their mind. I say: "I could go into an entire Derren Brown-style routine, getting you to think of colours, shapes, values, images, and so on, or … I could just tell you that you have the two of hearts" (which they do). At this stage I interject quickly before they do anything embarrassing such as applaud.
>
> "You remember I said the secret is often childishly simple? Well that's very much the case here, because these cards are all the two of hearts … except for the one that I allowed you to see on the bottom of the pack." As everyone lets out a joint groan I explain that even with a trick as simple as this a variety of the Rules of Magic come into play.

Rule 3, for instance: ***Communication can only register effectively when it builds on what the audience already knows.*** I can use playing cards to communicate with you because everyone is familiar with playing cards. It probably wouldn't work so well with, say, Tarot cards – most people are unfamiliar with concepts such as "major arcana". It reminds me of a business example where many years ago I heard a talk by Bill Gates. Essentially he was telling us that we would soon be using PDAs, but he didn't use that term, nor Personal Digital Assistants, not even Palm Pilots – it would not have registered with us as they had yet to be invented. Instead, he described it as "a sort of electronic wallet", so enabling us to get our minds around the size and shape, where we would keep it and how we would use it – he was basing his communication on what we already knew.

The most important rule is **Rule 1** – ***The framework for any communication is determined by the expectations and perceptions that you trigger.*** The moment I take out the cards it opens up a file in everyone's brains, telling them what they already know about playing cards – 52 cards, four suits, two colours and so on – and shutting out what doesn't fit, such as the possibility of them all being the same. So magicians can be confident that by using key words and actions their audience is all geared up to take in their message.

Once you have assessed what "files" you are opening, **Rule 2** comes into play. ***Expectations and perceptions can be reinforced or diminished by Prestige, Atmosphere & Environment and Desire.*** In this case I have told everyone I am a member of the world famous

Magic Circle (Prestige) and I have described the scenario within the club (Atmosphere & Environment); with judgment and a little luck I have also selected a volunteer who enjoys magic (Desire).

I explain that many of the rules are essentially very simple and it is magic that helps to bring them alive. **Rule 5,** for instance – ***Concentrated attention requires a single point of focus*** – is something I had always known. But during 20 years in PR it never hit home quite so clearly as when I heard the Canadian magician Gary Kurtz (who trained as a psychologist) say: "Don't divide attention between yourself and what you are doing." I demonstrate how in magic that means things like avoiding doing card tricks at arm's length. Immediately people start to look at the cards in my outstretched hands and I point out that their attention is now flitting between my face and my groin of all places; and you don't really want to create focus down there! It's much better to bring the cards up close to the face, so creating a Single Point of Focus. In business presentations you want to keep close in to any props or screen. You also want to start planning how to simplify your messages so that you create Single Points of Focus mentally as well as physically.

Having created a Single Point of Focus you can benefit from applying **Rule 6 – *Attention tracks from left to right, then settles at the left.*** This is because in Western cultures we read that way. So I always set myself and any visual aids or screen left-to-right from the audience's point of view. That way they will look at me, look across to my aids and then their attention will naturally revert to me.

Rule 18 – *Doubts are reduced by openness but may be increased by over-stressing* also applies in the scenario of my silly trick. Magicians will always be saying "pick a card, any card, do you want to change your mind and so on" – showing much openness so as to reduce the suspicion they might be cheating. What they need to avoid is phrases like "I have here a perfectly ordinary pack of cards." Such over-stressing is more likely to raise suspicion than avert it. In business the equivalent might be "Feel free to speak with any one of our clients." In reality there might be one or two who are best avoided, but by appearing so open they should inspire confidence.

Finally, **Rule 19 – *People put more reliance on something they have worked out for themselves.*** When I am supposedly reading their minds for the two of hearts I allow them to see the different bottom card. So, even if only subconsciously, they are registering the fact that they can see a different card, which confirms in their minds that everything seems to be in order. Your brain will believe anything that you tell it, but it will question anything that anyone else tells it. So if you can communicate through persuasion, you have your audience locked in and ready to receive your message.

When I am coaching PR people I point out that it is this principle that makes PR so effective. Rather than "sell, sell, sell" good PR is floating the message or product in front of the right people at the right time and allowing them to come to their own conclusion.

Presentation Magic

This book is based on the coaching that I give to teams and individuals from all walks of business life. Their needs are broad ranging and include pitching for business, making important announcements to employees, facing their shareholders, addressing awards panels and persuading special interest groups, as well as selling. For a typical session I would introduce them to the principles of The Rules of Magic along the lines above and then ask them to do a short business presentation which I critique and we all discuss, so that everyone learns from each other's strengths and weaknesses.

At lunch time I often send the people I am coaching off to learn a magic trick – usually tailored to their company or organization – which I ask them to present during the afternoon. I do this for a number of reasons but primarily because a magic trick is rather like an entire presentation compressed into a few minutes, so there is much that can be learned in terms of opening, closing, building to a climax, managing audience participation and handling visual aids. Many people say this was the most useful part of the day because it took them out of their comfort zone and they learned so many useful principles.

The other major benefit of asking them to present a magic trick is that it can bring out useful and attractive personality traits that sometimes remain hidden when delivering a business presentation. Some people can be very stiff and formal when delivering a business presentation and, even if their colleagues encourage them to "lighten up", they protest that: "My clients expect me to be like this because, after all, I'm looking after their money." When they come to present their magic trick, however, their whole body language changes; there is a smile on their face which you can hear in their voice; they are telling us about themselves so you warm to them. As a result what they say comes over as more convincing. They can see and feel the effect for themselves, so the objective then becomes to apply at least a little of that approach in their business presentation so they will engage their audience much more effectively.

Training days usually conclude with group discussions on how they will adapt their presentations and presentation style in the future. Sometimes it is a matter of small but very significant and impactful tweaks. On other occasions it is more of a revelation. I have had feedback such as: "It's as though cataracts have been removed from their eyes; there is a new catchphrase in the office which goes Nick would never allow that."

This book is based on the coaching I give in those sessions. It combines the experience of 20 years pitching and presenting on a regular basis as a PR consultant with much that I have learned as a member of the world's foremost magic club plus fresh knowledge and experience from all around me on a daily basis. The main body of the book is divided into three equally important sections: we start with *Construction* before going anywhere near *Preparation* or *Delivery.*

PART I

CONSTRUCTION

Part I starts by considering the often under-appreciated importance of investing time in the building blocks of your presentation. Then we look at each of those building blocks in turn – the elements of *Construction* that will help you first to engage your audience then retain their attention while building to a climax. Along the way we shall supplement these elements with injections of impact and conviction. Only by addressing all of these factors at the *Construction* stage can you be sure of success when you come to *Delivery*.

One stylistic note before we start. I refer throughout the book to any person or people you might be addressing as an "audience". If this sounds a little theatrical, I make no apologies; it is by carefully considered planning that you are going to win over your audience and, arguably, the smaller your audience the more carefully considered that planning needs to be.

Chapter 1
THE IMPORTANCE OF INVESTING TIME IN CONSTRUCTION

JUST AS THE BUILDER CANNOT BUILD A HOUSE WITHOUT BRICKS AND OTHER MATERIALS, TOGETHER WITH A PLAN OF WHERE, HOW AND WHEN THEY GO TOGETHER, THE MAGICIAN ALSO NEEDS A CONSTRUCTION PROCESS TO CREATE A MAGICAL EXPERIENCE. THE "BRICKS" FOR THE MAGICAL PROCESS INCLUDE ATTENTION, EMPATHY, INTRIGUE, PACING, CONVINCERS AND FOCUS. LAYING THESE BRICKS IN THE RIGHT AMOUNTS AND AT THE MOST APPROPRIATE MOMENTS REQUIRES METICULOUS PLANNING.

All too often training in presentation skills puts too much emphasis on *Delivery* and very little, if any, on the two other essential elements: *Construction* and *Preparation*.

Help with *Delivery* is what delegates have come to expect from training in presentation skills, and often that is the extent of what is provided. You will frequently find that the trainers are actors who bring their own agendas on how to breathe, how to stand, how to flex the vocal chords. Along with all this, great importance is placed on videoing each delegate's delivery and that brings with it camera crews, technical difficulties and endless playbacks.

Now, all these things *are* important, but I believe very strongly that *Construction* carries equal importance to *Delivery*. Here's a little secret that I am happy to reveal up front: if you get the *Construction* right, *Delivery* becomes so much easier. The reason for this is that time invested in *Construction* brings a proper ordering to the content, paring it back to the essentials and resulting in a natural flow that matches the rhythms and nuances of the speaker.

I was once called in for a one-to-one coaching session with the head of human resources at a leading financial services company. The brief was apparently straightforward: "I have to get up in front of the whole company at the local sports stadium and announce far-reaching structural changes. And I'm terrified." What she probably anticipated from me was a big focus on controlling nerves, handling difficult questions and avoiding specific danger areas. What I actually did was to lay a printed version of her slides on a large table, having observed a rather shaky initial run through of her early draft presentation. I re-ordered a number of the slides and simplified everything, partly by discarding some of the slides altogether. "Try it like this," I said to my new client, who was looking somewhat taken aback that I had seemingly pulled her presentation apart. What followed was a much more succinct and confidently delivered presentation, which sparked a few further tweaks of her own. By the third run through she declared: "I'm not frightened anymore because it now has a natural flow to it. I feel I am speaking from my heart and I'm not having to continually worry about what comes next." So the original brief was covered quite quickly, giving us plenty of time to focus on how to add impact to the presentation, how to make the most effective use of the space and ways to make it more engaging and even interactive.

So getting the *Construction* right makes *Delivery* easier, as well as making the presentation more effective. This story also points to the benefit of using a third party to help you. When it comes to *Construction* you will often find that the right content is already there, but it needs re-ordering and editing. We will look at editing in more detail later, specifically at the need to be ruthless – "killing your darlings", as they say in the film business. The objective viewpoint of someone who is not so close to the subject matter can be invaluable in this area.

Video cameras

As a footnote to the issue of using video to train people in presentation skills, I do believe that trainers can be too quick to summon their video crews without considering the pros and cons. Although video cameras are pretty ubiquitous these days, many of us still don't really like being caught on camera. The effect of having every personal nuance considered and your skin complaint magnified across the boardroom screen in a room full of colleagues can be excruciating. I have been called into some companies specifically because their staff had been traumatized by previous experiences with actors accompanied by video crews – particularly companies with young and inexperienced trainees. You have to ask what you are hoping to achieve by videoing those being trained. Of course, there is a good argument to suggest that using video recording is useful for experienced presenters seeking to iron out a few wrinkles and perfect their performance. But few people are actually going to be presenting on television, so coming over well on TV is not really relevant, and the mechanics may simply unnerve them.

Happily, there is actually a good magical precedent for training without video cameras. Legendary magician Tommy Cooper used to advise his show business friends against rehearsing in front of a mirror. When his friends expressed surprise at this – after all, magicians do have to check the angles of view with certain tricks – Cooper explained that if you rehearse in front of a mirror you put too much attention on yourself rather than on the audience, who should be your real focus. I discussed this with leading magician Geoffrey Durham who agreed with Cooper and went a stage further by pointing out that by rehearsing in front of a mirror your eyes are going to become fixed in one position and at the wrong level to engage with most of the audience.

In a nutshell

Time invested in *Construction* makes your presentation better in terms of content and structure. It also makes it easier to present and enables you to be a great presenter.

Chapter 2
ENGAGEMENT

*Assessing the expectations and perceptions you trigger,
then making them work for you; building on what your
audience already knows; adjusting your messages to create
empathy; making your message important to your audience;
deciding on the best approach; tools of engagement –
PowerPoint and its alternatives*

2.1 Expectations and perceptions

MAGICIANS APPROACH A POTENTIAL AUDIENCE ALMOST
PAINFULLY AWARE THAT THE MERE MENTION OR SIGHT
OF A MAGICIAN IS GOING TO TRIGGER A WHOLE SERIES OF
MEMORIES AND PERCEPTIONS, RANGING FROM POSITIVELY
WARM AND WONDROUS TO THOSE THEY WOULD PREFER TO
FORGET. THEY NEED TO IDENTIFY THE PERCEPTIONS THEY ARE
TRIGGERING AND WORK QUICKLY TO CAPITALIZE ON POSITIVES
AND OVERCOME NEGATIVES.

Our brains are self-organizing – they automatically sort data, working
like a huge filing system, storing information logically for easy retrieval.
New information is classified by comparing it with what is already "on
file" via our memory. The relevant file then opens and interprets what
we are seeing, hearing or taking in through other senses.

So you should always consider: What "files" am I opening in the
minds of my audience? As they look you up and down – probably
before you have said or done anything – what are they likely to be
thinking? That you look a bit old/young? Smart/scruffy? Expert-like?
"One of us"? As with any first-impressions situation, a myriad of

thoughts will be flitting through your audience's minds and these will form the framework for your communication.

Arguably the most important of all the Rules of Magic is:

Rule 1 – The framework for your communication is determined by the expectations and perceptions that you trigger

Think back to the pack of cards that I described in the Introduction. As soon as I took them out it opened files in the minds of the audience, telling them what they already knew about playing cards – 52 cards, all different, and so on. The reality – that all except the bottom card were the same – was actually shut out of their minds by the expectations I triggered, so setting me up to do a very easy bit of pretend mind reading.

Back in the real world, the best example is probably politicians. When they are seeking election they do all they can to persuade us that their policies are the best for the nation, but their appearance and personalities count for so much of the decision we take when we come to vote. When British Prime Minister David Cameron was seeking election to the leadership of the Conservative Party he was little known, so first impressions were going to count for a lot. As we prepared to hear his ideas for the future of the party and the policies he proposed, the scene was set by a range of perceptions or "files" opening up in our minds: *young, inexperienced, quite good looking, privileged upbringing, nice-looking wife, young children including one who was handicapped.* His opponent David Davis, by comparison, sparked thoughts such as: *middle aged, more experienced, self-made, rugged looks including a broken nose, and a wife who looked more dependable than destined for fashion features.* None of this had any real bearing on their ability to run the party, let alone the country, but all of it set the tone for the decisions we would make when it came to election time.

In 2010 British politician Alan Johnson was expected to stand for leadership of the Labour Party, after its defeat in the general election. He declined to do so, despite having much experience and support from leading members who saw him, with his working class and orphanage background, as the perfect foil to the Old Etonian now leading the Conservative Party. Johnson explained his decision not to stand by saying: "The candidates all come from a certain mould. It's the same mould that Cameron and Clegg come from. I suppose it would have added a bit of grit to the debate if I'd been there too, but it would all have been about my background, not about what I was saying."

Elections in the USA have always been more personality-led than in the UK because of the presidential system. In recent years US elections have seen the candidates grappling with perception issues including *black/white, male/female, young and inexperienced/ experienced and potentially too old.*

So you need to consider what files you are opening in the minds of your audience, and you need to think specifically in terms of the prejudices they might hold and to what extent their knowledge and experience might be limited.

Working with the perceptions you trigger
Once you have made these assessments your attention should turn to how you can build on the resulting perceptions or, if necessary, play them down.

> **Rule 2** – Expectations and perceptions can be reinforced or diminished by Prestige, Atmosphere & Environment and Desire

In my introductory patter I talk of my Magic Circle membership (Prestige), the magicians in the HQ bar (Atmosphere & Environment) and I always play the magic up or down according the interest they have indicated up front (Desire).

A placebo is a good example of the principle working in the real world. A placebo is officially prescribed by a doctor (Prestige) who operates from a surgery – a building dedicated to making people better (Atmosphere & Environment) – and the patient wants to get better (Desire), so they do.

The issue that most frequently needs addressing through Rule 2 in my training sessions is that of age. Many of the people I coach are highly qualified in a field such as healthcare or finance, but they are often quite young and some look younger than their actual age. This triggers expectations and perceptions that are unhelpful to the development of a working relationship with a client paying a lot of money for expertise and advice. Whether or not the client voices such feelings, the consultants with youthful looks feel at a disadvantage, creating a nervousness that undermines them further. The solution is to build in elements of Prestige, Atmosphere & Environment and Desire at an early stage – essentially, carefully woven name dropping about places they have been and people they know, so finding common ground that helps to accelerate mutual respect.

The Desire card is also an important one to play. During my time in public relations I had certain clients who continued to live with the rather old-fashioned belief that you needed first to be a journalist in order to be really effective in PR. I tended not to employ journalists, but when I did I urged them to emphasize their journalistic credentials. This made for happy clients in certain instances and it also boosted the confidence of journalists-turned-PRs, who often felt a little uncomfortable when they first swapped trades.

Having assessed the expectations and perceptions that you are triggering, and done your best to make them work for you, the next move is to:

2.2   **Building on what your audience already knows**

MAGICIANS USE PLAYING CARDS FOR A VARIETY OF REASONS, BUT PRIMARILY BECAUSE THEY PROVIDE A SET OF 52 DIFFERENT OBJECTS THAT ARE HIGHLY PORTABLE, INSTANTLY RECOGNIZABLE AND UNDERSTOOD THROUGHOUT THE CIVILIZED WORLD.

MAGIC SURVIVES IN A HI-TECH WORLD AFTER THOUSANDS OF YEARS, PARTLY BECAUSE OF THE RISE OF "STREET MAGIC" – MAGIC PERFORMED ON THE STREET, IN YOUR HANDS, USING EVERYDAY OBJECTS, RATHER THAN GAUDILY PAINTED PROPS.

The fast track to engaging your audience is to base your communication on what they already know, using familiar reference points that open up "files" within their minds.

In my Introduction I use playing cards because they are a set of objects that are familiar to everyone, traverse language barriers and trigger a series of expectations and perceptions that I can play with. I also mention the business example of Bill Gates successfully communicating the principles of PDAs prior to their launch. A good example of *un*successful communication – certainly in the case of the UK audience – was the launch of another technological innovation a few years later. Tivo marked a real milestone in the recording of TV programmes, yet within two years of its announcement in the UK it had closed down its British operations, leaving Sky Plus to pick up the baton some years later. I believe the failure of Tivo's communication to engage its audience played a big part in its failure.

Slogans such as "You can freeze live TV" were messages that the audience found difficult to get their minds around. The concept was alien to TV viewers – it simply didn't seem credible that you could freeze live TV– so they needed education, both about the technology and the ways in which it would prove useful. Even "It's like having your own TV station" was a stretch too far; with a few exceptions, such as Rupert Murdoch, no one actually had their own

TV station, so it wasn't something many people thought about or aspired to. Pausing and rewinding live TV is now a facility that we all use, so Tivo was ahead of its time. It might have done better to start by focusing on what we were actually thinking. It used to be something of a cliché that no one really knew how to operate their video recorder, so there was great potential for messages along the lines of "Never miss another episode," "One click and you have the whole series recorded," and so on.

Top Gear presenter Jeremy Clarkson and comedy writer and performer Catherine Tate are two high-profile experts at *building on what their audiences already know*. One of Clarkson's tricks is to use similes, and he now admits that this dates back to his early days in motoring journalism when he didn't actually know very much about cars. In order to go into any depth he needed to make allusions to topics such as food or sex, and he soon found that he was attracting an audience that went way beyond the usual petrolheads. So he stuck with the technique and went on to become one of the BBC's biggest stars with lucrative sidelines in journalism and publishing.

Much of Catherine Tate's success in creating comedy characters can be attributed to the fact that we know old ladies like her Granny character and we come across surly teenagers with an "Am I bovvered?" attitude. Accordingly, Tate says that in order for comedy to be successful it has to be: "Eight parts recognition, one part shock and one part exaggeration." Gross exaggeration is, of course, another weapon in Clarkson's arsenal.

Building on what your audience already knows can be taken a stage further by considering how to create empathy:

2.3 Creating empathy

FEW MAGICIANS THESE DAYS HAVE THE LUXURY OF AN ORCHESTRA PIT TO PUT SPACE BETWEEN THEM AND THEIR AUDIENCE. IN MANY SITUATIONS THEY HAVE TO CREATE MAGIC

WHERE AND WHEN THEY CAN, AND THAT OFTEN MEANS ON
THE STREET OR TABLE HOPPING AT BANQUETS. AUDIENCE
FEEDBACK IS THEREFORE INSTANT AND OFTEN BRUTALLY
HONEST, MEANING THAT MAGICIANS BECOME HIGHLY ADEPT
AT ADJUSTING THEIR APPROACH TO SUIT EACH INDIVIDUAL
AUDIENCE, OFTEN MANY TIMES A NIGHT.

Consider what needs adjusting to more closely suit your audience:

Jargon

Might anyone in your audience fail to understand the language you
are using? In the right circumstances, jargon can actually be helpful
in terms of developing a bond with your audience, but it should be
avoided if there is a risk that even one person does not understand
the words and thereby feels excluded.

Relevance and Complexity

Does the detail of your communication need simplifying or
modifying for a specific audience on a particular occasion? Too often
people simply launch into their usual speech with little regard for the
audience they are addressing. Former British Prime Minister Tony
Blair received a rough ride – including slow hand claps – quite late in
his premiership when he addressed the Women's Institute. I once saw
a mayor talking about budgets and votes to *children*.

As with most cases, these two examples needed only relatively
small adjustments to their regular speeches in order to match the
needs and interests of their audiences. The mayor could have engaged
the children's attention by asking them about the local facilities –
parks, swimming pools and so on – that they enjoy before giving
them a brief insight into what goes into providing those facilities.
Blair, meanwhile, could probably have got away with a quick edit of
his policy statements by his adviser on women's issues.

Often it comes down to a question of the age of the audience, and magicians are acutely aware of the adjustments required. To give a simple example, those card tricks that I said could be used universally are a non-starter for children; they have yet to develop perceptions and associations about packs of cards, so finding the three of clubs means nothing to them, how ever clever your technique.

One of the stories that I use for my own training – and which I intend to share with my readers later – centres around the legendary performance at *Live Aid* in 1985 by rock band Queen. I only use it, however, if I am speaking to a middle-aged audience because, no matter how well it illustrates a key point, to anyone under 40 it's simply a piece of ancient history!

Cultural references

If the people, places and incidents you are using for illustration are not recognized by your audience you will fail in your bid to clarify your point and may even end up confusing them.

Magicians are quite fortunate in this respect, in that magic is a fairly universal language. But it is noticeable that few comedians cross borders successfully, even when they share the same language. Eddie Izzard is one of the few British comedians who have found success in different countries, and even different languages, and he is scrupulous in researching for empathy matches. If, for instance, he wants to talk about a chocolate bar – or candy bar as his American audiences would have it – he makes it a KitKat because he has established that this brand is widely available in the territories that he covers.

I found myself booked to work in Swaziland a few years ago. So, needing to practise what I preach, I started researching the cultural references that would be familiar in that part of southern Africa. Looking into which movie stars they favour, my first Google search for "cinema in Swaziland" produced a quote from Richard E Grant stating: "There is no cinema in Swaziland." Bad start, I thought.

How am I going to find any common ground if I can't even use my Tom Cruise stories? Happily, Richard E Grant provided the answer as well as the conundrum; he had recently made a film *Wah-Wah* which included my friend Celia Imrie in the cast. I called Celia who first advised me to watch the film, which I had to admit I had missed, and then filled me in on the blanks.

Sex

It may sound old fashioned to adjust your messages according to whether you are addressing men or women, but they do have different motivators and they take in information in rather different ways. Like so many things, this is a lesson that I learned the hard way and from an unlikely source.

Before he found fame on TV I hired comedian and impressionist Alistair McGowan to entertain my staff at a Christmas party. He turned up early at the venue in a London pub and as he peeped through the door to assess the audience and the performing space he said: "Hey Nick, I wish you'd told me you've got so many women." When I asked why, he reminded me that so much of his material was about sport and he was concerned that my staff would not recognize the voices. So we sat down and methodically went through his set list, deciding to include the cat sketch, the weatherman and some DJs, but to steer clear of the football commentators. He went down a storm and probably would have done so with his standard set, but here again you get instant feedback when working as a comedian and he had clearly had a few specific learning experiences along the way.

It is rather crude psychology, but a broad rule of thumb is that while men respond well to facts and statistics, women prefer stories, anecdotes and metaphors. And the Alistair McGowan incident points to one way that men can learn to communicate more effectively with women in the work place, which is to call "time out" on the sporting metaphors. Men slip all too easily into peppering their talk with sports-based phrases such as "raise the bar", "go the distance", and "step up to the plate", which are just a little too macho to really motivate or even connect with many women.

Having considered all the factors that could help to create empathy with your audience, the next step is to make your message important to them:

2.4 Making your message important to your audience

MAGICIANS ARE ACUTELY AWARE OF THE POWER THAT COMES FROM MAKING THEIR MESSAGE IMPORTANT TO THEIR AUDIENCE. IF THEY MAKE THEIR HANDKERCHIEF DISAPPEAR OR DO SOME CLEVER COIN MANIPULATIONS THEY WILL PROBABLY RECEIVE SOME POLITE APPLAUSE; IF, HOWEVER, THEY BORROW A WATCH FROM A MEMBER OF THE AUDIENCE, THEY GAIN MUCH CLOSER ATTENTION BECAUSE THE AUDIENCE HAS A PERSONAL INVOLVEMENT – AND INVESTMENT – IN THE PROCESS. WHAT'S MORE, THEY ARE ALL THE MORE LIKELY TO TALK ABOUT IT AFTERWARDS.

At the crux of this stage is:

Rule 4 – The brain filters out most of the information it receives, leaving only what it considers important

Psychologists argue about the amount of information the brain takes in every single second – I have seen estimates ranging from 500 pieces of information to as much as 11 million. What they are generally agreed upon is that the brain can only retain a small percentage of that information; it can manage somewhere between 16 and 40 pieces at any one time. So there is a big disparity that is exacerbated by modern life, in which marketing messages bombard us through multi-media 24 hours a day. It has been suggested that more information has been produced in the past 30 years than in the previous 5,000 years.

Think about when you have chosen a new car or perhaps changed your mobile phone. You have probably devoted time and careful consideration to your decision and may even be congratulating yourself on the select nature of your choice. And then suddenly you seem to see that model everywhere. That's because it has become *important* to you. I had exactly this experience when my car was due its annual MOT (road worthiness test). The local testing centre I had used for some years had closed down and I cursed the fact that I would have to go in search of another and fretted over how inconvenient it would be getting to and from an alternative supplier, once I had found one. I decided to peer down some alleys near my home in case there was a test centre I'd failed to spot in the past. What actually happened was that I pulled out into the main road, just around the corner from the house I'd been living for nine years, and 50 metres on the right was a giant sign saying "MOT tests and all your motoring needs." I had been driving past this sign for nearly a decade – it was even on the school run – and yet it had never registered with me before because an MOT test had not been important to me. Now that it had become important, the sign loomed large.

This is how people and objects can remain "hidden in plain sight"; they blend in so well with the surroundings that they become effectively invisible. As Rule 15 says: *Over-familiarity leads to "invisibility"*. The "watch test" demonstrates this very well. It's an old favourite with magicians, but this version is by former president of The Magic Circle David Berglas. Known as the International Man of Mystery, David is the guru and hero to many magicians including Derren Brown, who described him as "One of our greatest living magical performers." David has done much work outside the performance arena, including training police recruits at Hendon in observation techniques.

This is exactly as he described the watch test to me; you might like to try it for yourself.

> **Without looking, tell me if your watch has Roman or Arabic numerals, or maybe dashes or dots?**
>
> Incredible as it may seem, many people do not know the answer, despite the fact that they are looking at their watch all day, every day. Allow them to look to check their answer, then ask:

> **How is the three/six position marked on your watch?**
>
> In spite of having just looked at their watch, many people are unsure or incorrect, having failed to register that a date indicator or other device actually fills this position. Allow them to look to check their answer, then ask:

> **Has it got a second hand?**
>
> Some people will even be unsure about this, but if they answer with great confidence ask them a further question:

> **Does it move in steps or a sweep motion?**
>
> Allow them to look to check their answer, then ask:

> **Finally, what time is it?**
>
> They have just looked at their watch two or three times and yet most people will be unable to tell you the time – it simply failed to register. As David Berglas says: "You looked but you didn't see."

One final point on the watch test. Those with Roman numerals on their watch will probably be more likely to answer correctly because of the distinctive design – they may have chosen it specifically for the

Roman numerals. If so, ask them to draw the way the 4 appears on their watch face. They are most likely to draw a IV because that is the convention we are used to and yet most 4s on watches with Roman numerals appear as IIII.

Making a message important through personalization

You need to *make* your message important to your audience and the most direct route is to personalize your message to them – get straight onto their favourite subject. Magicians will therefore seek to borrow items from the audience, produce a relevant gift and create climaxes that involve the company logo or the birthday girl's name.

My own magical performances are confined mainly to topping and tailing my talks and illustrating points in my training, but I like to have my arm twisted occasionally for events such as fundraisers at the children's schools, as it keeps my real world experience up to date. Typically, the events have a theme or specific focus which lend themselves well to personalization and I find myself getting fantastic reactions to tricks that would normally seem mundane and which I simply wouldn't consider performing without the element of personalization.

Imagine the scenario: I am at a fundraising event for the local school and I show some cards from which we eliminate selections one by one until only the Three of Clubs is left; that matches a prediction I made earlier and furthermore it is the only red-backed card among an otherwise blue-backed stack. Quite clever, but so what? And it's hardly the sort of thing anyone is going to be talking about over the water cooler tomorrow. Imagine now that I have a set of cards bearing pictures of individual teachers rather than playing-card imagery; suddenly it becomes altogether more interesting with everyone hoping their favourite will be the chosen one. In-jokes are enjoyed as selections are discarded and then the winner turns out to be the only one with the school's crest on the back. It's the same trick but it's so much more involving and meaningful to all concerned, so they play along throughout, enjoy it and are still talking about it the next day.

2.5 Deciding on the best approach

"Do you like card tricks?"

"No, I hate card tricks," I answered.

"Well, I'll just show you this one."

He showed me three.

I did not like Mr. Kelada.

Extract from "Mr. Know All"
by W Somerset Maugham

What approach will this particular audience respond to best? Would they appreciate a dramatic, "all-singing, all-dancing" type of presentation or are they more the sort of people who would say: "Never mind all that, just give me the facts." This can be difficult to judge. Often it is people in more hum-drum jobs who like to be perked up by a little razzamataz. Those working in a more cutting-edge environment probably feel they have seen it all before and may appreciate more of a plain-vanilla approach.

Then, will they respond best to concise information or are they fine-detail people? Part of this comes down to the way individuals within your audience take in information. Each will have their own preferred thinking style and, while the majority of people are likely be primarily visual thinkers, some will respond better to auditory information while others are likely to be moved most by kinesthetic information based on feelings and emotions.

> Visual thinkers think in pictures, are very aware of colours and how things look, and they talk fast with language such as "Let me draw you a picture …"

Auditory thinkers are very aware of sound, are easily distracted and talk more slowly in phrases such as "Have you heard about …"

Kinesthetic thinkers' thoughts are based around body sensations and they are very aware of how things feel – clothes, seating, light and so on. They tend to speak slowly in terms such as "Are you comfortable with that?" and "Let's press some flesh."

Clearly this is a whole subject in itself, but the key point is that by matching your communication approach to your audience's preferred thinking style you can establish real rapport quite rapidly. Often you will find it easiest to establish what is *not* the preferred thinking style of a particular person. I have a long-standing client who is the multi-millionaire founder of a financial services company. Yet, I have seen him literally put his head in his hands when faced by two sheets of paper full of small print. I have also witnessed him look like a frightened rabbit when asked to do a simple mental sum. Show him a diagram, however, or describe something in graphic terms and his face lights up.

When it comes to presentation, the big challenge is that your audience members are likely to have a range of different preferred thinking styles, so remember:

Rule 12 – The senses offer five different ways into the brain

To reach every member of your audience to best effect you need to stimulate as many senses as possible. In addition to visual, auditory and kinesthetic, there is also olfactory (smell) and gustatory (taste). The first three are undoubtedly the most readily usable, but keep in mind that smell and taste are highly evocative. Think for a moment of lemons. I don't know how powerful lemon extract really is as a cleaning agent, but anything that has been cleaned with a lemon-based detergent certainly gives the impression of being super clean. Now imagine you are biting into a lemon and the juice is seeping slightly out of the corners of your mouth; I bet your taste buds are tingling already.

Finally, in terms of approach, what sort of media will your audience respond to best? Do they expect a PowerPoint presentation? Or might they prefer something more informal? If they do expect a PowerPoint presentation, then presenting *without* PowerPoint just could be the best thing to do because it will make you stand out. On the other hand, it might just irritate them. Again, much of this comes down to the preferred thinking styles of your audience members, but you must consider this: regardless of what you usually do, what will create the best impact for this audience in this situation?

It's time to choose your Tools of Engagement.

2.6   Tools of engagement

BIG PRODUCTIONS WILL ALWAYS HAVE THEIR PLACE, AND MAGICIANS ARE PARTICULARLY DRAWN TO THE GLAMOUR AND GLITZ OF LAS VEGAS. EQUALLY, THEY KNOW THAT THE STRONGEST MAGIC OF ALL IS OFTEN ACHIEVED WITH THE MINIMUM OF PROPS OR STAGING.

The important starting point here is to remember that the main tools of engagement – your voice, eyes and body – come from within. We shall come to those later in the *Delivery* section. At the *Construction* stage the focus should be on selecting the most suitable technology, deciding how much technology to use and, indeed, whether to use technology at all. So let's start with "the big one", then follow by considering alternatives and the option of mixed media.

PowerPoint
There is a multitude of statistics to support the importance of the visual element in a presentation. Some of these should be taken

with a large pinch of salt as their provenance has been lost and their meaning twisted, but typically it is suggested that information is relayed to the brain as follows: 83% comes via the eyes, 11% via the ears and 6% via other senses. In terms of retaining information, verbal stimulus may account for as little of as 10%, compared with 50% for visuals.

Let's not worry too much about numbers; the point is that visuals can make a great contribution to most presentations in terms of engagement, clarification and enhancement. The problem is that the default method of building visual aids into presentations – the ubiquitous Microsoft PowerPoint – can create many more problems than it solves. "Death by PowerPoint" has become a cliché that is all too familiar, certainly in business and increasingly in the classroom and the church hall as well. I always urge the people I am coaching to understand that you don't *have* to use PowerPoint; there are other ways to help you communicate and those may even be more appropriate in certain situations. The fact is, though, that in many situations we are expected to present with PowerPoint and you may need to be rather brave to both go against expectations and manage without what may have come to feel like a rather comfortable crutch.

Installed on hundreds of millions of computers around the world, Microsoft PowerPoint accounts for around 95% of the presentation market. It has been estimated that some 30 million PowerPoint presentations are delivered every day. And yet to many people in business PowerPoint has become almost a dirty word and the prospect of a PowerPoint presentation can spark a feeling of dread. Increasingly, those with the authority to make such decisions are imposing "No PowerPoint" policies.

Personally, I believe PowerPoint can be a wonderful tool, but people forget that it's a *tool* – a tool to *support them as a speaker*, rather than an end in itself. "*You* are the show," I say to those I am coaching, "PowerPoint has a supporting role, at best." Unfortunately, the problem is getting worse because there are now whole generations of presenters for whom PowerPoint is all they have ever known.

To use PowerPoint properly you need to start by understanding the pitfalls that it puts in the path of any presenter. My own personal investigations point to seven specific deadly sins:

1st *Deadly Sin* – PowerPoint steals attention from you as a speaker

It – rather than you – becomes the focus and the eye contact that is so essential to true engagement is never properly established, let alone maintained. Too often PowerPoint slides contain far too many words, so that attention is on reading words – or *trying* to read them in the worst cases – rather than paying attention to you. And unless you use animation to bring points up one at a time, PowerPoint steals your thunder – the audience is reading ahead rather than listening to the point you are making now. You are failing to achieve the Single Point of Focus demanded by Rule 5.

2nd *Deadly Sin* – PowerPoint makes the format rigid

The format appears to be locked in – there seems to be no flexibility to suit specific audience reactions and the mood of the moment. Someone might raise a particular point during the presentation and the presenter invariably feels powerless to do anything besides plead that their point will be coming up – in about 43 slides time, so please bear with me!

The format problem is exacerbated by the tendency for everything in PowerPoint to become a bunch of bullet points, which are not always the best way to communicate your messages. Various historic speeches have been turned into PowerPoint format to illustrate this failing; the one I use for my own training is Winston Churchill's legendary "We shall fight them on the beaches" speech. As I mimic Churchill with the various elements – beaches, landing grounds, hills – each coming up as a bullet point, but not quite in the rhythm of my speech, it is easy to demonstrate that PowerPoint is not always helpful; indeed, sometimes you are better off without it.

3rd Deadly Sin – PowerPoint puts "design" into the hands of amateurs

Everybody fiddles with the presentation, forcing in all they have to say with scant regard for any of the principles of good design. In the old pre-PowerPoint days we used 35mm slides and had to order these in from a specialist supplier, ensuring that at least there was one level of quality control. The Do-It-Yourself nature of PowerPoint means that anything goes.

4th Deadly sin – PowerPoint offers all things to all people

Probably the greatest sin of all and certainly the biggest troublemaker. PowerPoint can be used as a visual aid, a speaker prompt, a handout, a takeaway document, a standalone or mail-out document and probably a number of other uses besides. The trouble is that to do any of these jobs properly you really need a different treatment for each. Generally speaking, a slide makes a lousy handout and a handout makes a lousy slide. Even if people understand this, how many take the trouble to create different versions?

5*th Deadly Sin* – PowerPoint kills the art of business conversation

The format is such that we end up presenting *to* each other rather than discussing *with* each other. Furthermore, there is also an implied obligation to plough through all the slides until the bitter end, when sometimes it might actually be better to shut down the slides, having used them to stimulate interaction, and simply let the conversation flow.

It must also be said that PowerPoint enables weak content to be disguised. The format, layout and eye-catching animation can all too easily conspire to create a superficial sheen with the reality only truly coming to light once the presentation is over.

6*th Deadly Sin* – PowerPoint creates worry and stress around a mere mechanism

If you have to worry about anything – and a degree of nerves is generally a good thing – it should be about your personal delivery, not a support mechanism. The trouble is that so much of the focus of creating and preparing for a presentation goes into making sure "The PowerPoint Presentation" is right. Whole teams of people devote tremendous energy to writing it, editing and correcting it and then printing it out to look as beautiful and businesslike as possible. As the final page comes off the printer everyone heaves a huge sigh of relief declaring: "It's done!" Wrong! Where the real effort should go is on how you as people are going to engage other people; the PowerPoint is just a mechanism to help you do that – where applicable. *You* are the show; *it* has a supporting role, at best.

7th *Deadly Sin* – **PowerPoint makes everyone look the same**

Rule 15 states *Over-familiarity leads to invisibility*. To create impact you need to do something a bit different or else you risk blending into the background and becoming part of the furniture. Unfortunately PowerPoint works against you in this respect. While it is possible to make PowerPoint look like almost anything you want, few people have the skills, time or funds to achieve that, so their presentations end up looking remarkably similar to each other's. The problem is exacerbated by the many convenience features built into PowerPoint, automatically prompting layouts, colour schemes and fonts. You also need to bear in mind that PowerPoint acts as an anchor – the moment an audience gains a glimpse of the format it takes them back (Rule 1) to every PowerPoint presentation they have ever seen; not a good starting point.

So PowerPoint creates all sorts of problems – it can be a menace. Some people have given up on it altogether. I have a client with a "No PowerPoint" policy and it makes them distinctive and memorable because, typically, they have to present alongside five or six competitors, all heavily armed with PowerPoint.

That said, I reiterate my belief that PowerPoint can be a fantastic tool that, used correctly, can enhance all you do, even creating a "halo" effect for you as a speaker. Among the benefits it brings to the presenter are: it helps you deliver more content; enables subtle repetition; it allows Do-It-Yourself; it's speedy and cost effective; it's universally available and understood; it allows you to create take-away notes as you go. All of which may sound somewhat repetitive because the benefits are remarkably similar to the Seven Deadly Sins.

Of course it's good that it is speedy, cost-effective, universal and so on, but those can also be key to PowerPoint's downfall.

So success with PowerPoint comes down largely to the user: in the right hands and with proper forethought it can be a fantastic tool, especially in terms of delivering all-important visual information. We should still ask, nevertheless, how it ever got to the stage whereby the output of the tool that became ubiquitous for the business community, before invading schools, churches and so many other places, is known by such a derogatory term as Death by PowerPoint.

The guilty men

The guilty men are Dennis Austin and Bob Gaskins, who invented PowerPoint – initially called Presenter – back in 1987 before selling it to Microsoft for $14 million later that year. A few clues as to where it went so wrong can be gleaned from a look at the first ever PowerPoint presentation – the one the duo used to sell their new invention – which can still be found at Gaskins' web site www.robertgaskins.com. Take a look and you will see that it breaks just about every one of the presentation rules we used to learn before the days of PowerPoint. It's extremely dreary, packed with too much information and hard work to read off a page, let alone from a presentation screen. My belief is that too much emphasis went into the technology and not enough into best presentation practice, which is still very important, probably more so than ever now that PowerPoint brings the potential to actually work against you.

PowerPoint should support you, not drive you

The key to making PowerPoint work for you is to keep it in its proper place by remembering that *you* are the show and it has a mere supporting role. This should be obvious but is easily forgotten, and certainly came as something of a revelation to one highly experienced management consultant I was coaching. She was somewhat mystified that, after 30 years in business, her presentation skills seemed to have got worse rather than better. "I feel my personality becomes lost in the presentation and that creates a nervousness that I never used to have," she said.

As I watched her deliver her standard presentation it soon became clear that she was being *driven* by her PowerPoint rather than supported by it. Energy and concentration that should have been dedicated to engaging and empathizing with her audience were instead being diverted into worrying about what was coming on the next slide and when was the right time to change that slide. Furthermore, she was having to restrain her natural physical style of expression for fear of losing sight of her laptop prompt or standing too far in front of the screen. The attractive, engaging and energetic woman who had greeted me at the beginning of the day had turned into an efficient but slightly robotic presenter who had to be endured rather than enjoyed and had little to make her stand out or be remembered.

She knew she had not done well, but I sensed she was still a little mystified as to the reason. I could have explained her failings, but knew the impact would be much greater if she could work it out for herself (Rule 19 at play) so I made no comment. Instead I asked her to do it all again but without the PowerPoint. She looked at me aghast, as if to say: "How am I ever going to manage that?" I could see she was very familiar with her subject matter, so I gave her a gentle push. The moment she started, the attractive, engaging and energetic woman was back. I was drawn in and I actually wanted to hear what she had to say, despite already knowing the detail from the dull version. The point was that she was now in charge – she was being herself rather than being pushed along by her slides and the bullet point format that they dictate.

Importantly, it also helped to highlight where she could actually use a little help from PowerPoint. Together we picked out some visuals to convey a lot of information quickly: a couple of comparison charts where sets of data could be viewed side by side and a few bullet points to sum up her key messages in a way that hung together. So we didn't abandon the PowerPoint completely, we did a big editing job that cut out many of the words and left just the slides that supported her as a presenter. She was back in control – the PowerPoint beast had been tamed and made to do her bidding.

2.7 Alternatives to PowerPoint

If you are in any doubt as to whether PowerPoint is suitable for a specific presentation, or perhaps you suspect your presentation might work better without PowerPoint, my advice is as follows:

- Run through your draft presentation without any aids at all.
- Identify the places where you need help from visual aids of some kind.
- Consider what sort of aid would help in each instance and be really open-minded here, thinking in ideals. If, for instance, the presentation is about a car launch and you feel in an ideal world it would help to have that actual car in the room with you, then hold that thought (Saatchi & Saatchi actually did this once, so it's not necessarily impossible).
- If PowerPoint is needed at various points, you will feel it because you will be struggling to express what you really want to say.
- It may be, however, that alternative aids, such as props, pictures and participatory exercises, support your natural presentational style more appropriately – on this occasion.

There are legendary stories of people discovering their presentation was coming at the end of a long pitch process in which much PowerPoint had been featured. So they ditched their own PowerPoint and won the pitch – partly because the lack of PowerPoint made them stand out. I would like to think that Rule 13 – *Firsts and lasts are remembered* also had something to do with it.

Let's look at a few situations in which PowerPoint was given the day off:

The "bottle bank" pitch

Among the situations in which I have benefited from a different presentational approach was when my accountant advised me – for technical reasons – to apply for a new bank account for my PR business. He warned me that this may be difficult as I was in the midst of a complicated partnership change, but in order to impress the bank I should focus on the names of my famous blue chip clients. So I wrote the client names on a single sheet of paper, ready to show it to my potential new bank manager. Somehow it just didn't come over as impressively as it should have; the names were undeniably blue chip and famous, but they weren't jumping off the page.

So I decided to take my clients with me to the bank. I arrived with a large sports bag that I kept at my feet until the appropriate moment. Then I said: "Let me tell you who my clients are." And I reached into the bag for a bottle of Cockburn's Special Reserve port, which I put in front of him on the table. I followed with bottles of Harvey's Bristol Cream, Cockburn's LBV, Champagne Pommery, Holsten Pils, Babycham, Cherry B, Gaymer's Olde English Cider and packets of Typhoo tea and its many variants. Thinking back, it was reminiscent of Tommy Cooper's famous glass/bottle routine where he produces a series of Martini bottles from under a single tube, finishing with a whole table-full.

"As you can see," I said to the bank manager, "I have a lot of clients in the drinks industry and I also represent the Singapore Tourist Board, a national radio station ..." By now the table was full and he looked a little concerned as to what else I might produce from my bag, so he interrupted with an offer to open an account for me. I had made an impact with a table-full of bottles and I had "broken his pattern" – no one had ever communicated with him quite like that.

The pitch to Sir Richard Branson

An advertising agency was due to pitch to Sir Richard Branson. They went about preparing their pitch in the usual way until someone asked the key question: "Where will we be doing the pitch?" At Branson's place, came the answer, which got them thinking. It was common knowledge that Sir Richard had two large houses in London's Holland Park; he lived in one and worked in the other, but both had a very relaxed, residential style and feel to them. The team came to the conclusion they would probably be seated on sofas in a sitting room. PowerPoint with screens and projectors was going to feel out of place, jarring with the informal style for which Branson is so famous. So they took a framed picture of the celebrity they were recommending for the campaign and a sketchpad, much more appropriate to this situation – and they won the business.

The persuasive pitch to villagers in Swaziland

When I was on my training trip to Swaziland, I followed my usual routine of asking the delegates to bring a presentation they had done before, in whatever form they thought best suited that audience. One woman explained that her presentation was one that she did when visiting local communities in whatever was their usual meeting place, which could be almost anywhere and quite possibly outdoors. PowerPoint was clearly not going to be the preferred presentation tool. The objective, she explained, was to make the people in the communities understand the aid that they had received over the years and how they could put this to best use. The hidden agenda, she said, was to make them understand that they had been receiving increasing amounts over the years. This was, however, a sensitive issue and could not be said or discussed in an overt manner. What followed was one of the best and most effective presentations I have seen. She used some simple cards that showed the nature of the aid they had received each year, and she gradually stuck these to the wall, working left-to-right. By the time she had finished, the row of cards extended across the wall; what was left unsaid, but could be seen and perceived very clearly was that the line of cards rose as it went across the wall – like a graph depicting a progressive rise in revenues.

The lesson we can learn from such stories is that the straight answer to questions about the best approach to presentational tools and style is: "Whatever it takes to help you tell the story." So I hesitate to prescribe any standard alternatives, but let's at least consider the following:

Boards/flip-over paper charts

With desktop publishing these are much easier to produce than they were in days of old, but you need to ask yourself why you are using these rather than PowerPoint. Is it because you need something larger than a laptop screen but smaller than a projector screen? Is it because technology is not available or inappropriate to the situation?

Boards and charts are best used when:

- you have a limited number of boards (the more you have the more difficult they are to handle and transport).
- the boards contain mainly visual imagery.
- you know the exact size of room and audience numbers (you can't vary the size of the boards).
- you want to leave the boards on show, maybe so that your audience can compare a range of options.

While this latter reason is probably the best of all for using boards or charts, remember that in most situations you will be aiming for a Single Point of Focus rather than the potential distraction of a collection of different images.

Working through a document

Arguably the *worst* way to make a presentation, this can nevertheless be the expected norm in certain sectors such as finance, where audiences want the comfort of detailed data. The problems of working through a document are numerous and include lack of focus, the ability of the audience to jump ahead too soon to your big reveals and, above all, the near impossibility of maintaining any meaningful eye contact.

If working through a document is the expected norm in your situation it is probably wise not to fight this too hard. I have worked with clients in the finance sector to develop a way of having the best of both worlds. You can find this in Chapter 13.4 "Eye contact killers". My general advice with documents, however, is never to hand them out before the end, but give a very clear description upfront of what they can expect in their document so that they do not fret about the need to take detailed notes.

Flipcharts and whiteboards

There are some books on presentation techniques that make pronouncements such as "Flipcharts have no role in presentation." This alone makes me warm to the idea of using one. Indeed, many years ago a friend and I used to theorize about what would make the perfect presentation format and we eventually decided on a flipchart presentation where you appeared to make it up as you went along. The point was that it would be the most closely tailored presentation possible and it could include a lot of input from your audience; people were much more likely to buy the idea because they had been in on its creation. The reason that more orthodox presentation coaches dismiss the use of flipcharts is that it seems all too informal and ad hoc, but this is precisely why they can be used to advantage – if done carefully and sparingly.

In reality, of course, you would have prepared much of the presentation in advance and probably even have many key words already invisibly penciled in on the apparently blank flipchart sheets. Magicians are well versed in how much you can hide – in plain sight – with pencil markings on a flipchart sheet. This is what I call "white cheating"; it's like white lies – while you are cheating a little, you are doing it for the right reasons. You will find a section on White Cheating in the Appendix.

Old media – slide projector, cassette recorder, overhead projector

You would be hard pressed these days to come up with a good reason for using a carousel of 35mm slides, but if it helps you make your point, go for it. It is only a few years, however, since I last used a cassette recorder and the reason was that I was urging my trainees to keep their technological aids simple so as to avoid ambush. I had just watched a young PR executive first struggle to find the correct audio file on her computer, then make it audible over the laptop's tiny speakers. What was meant to enhance her presentation actually made it stall, leaving her flustered. As a suggested alternative I simply reached under the desk for a portable cassette player, pressed the play button and my tape rang out loud and clear. The beauty of old fashioned tape is that you can leave it ready and waiting cued in exactly the right place.

I can also imagine instances in which an overhead projector might be very suitable. Yes, there are hi-tech equivalents these days that allow you to write over your PowerPoint presentations and so on, but there is something delightfully reassuring and simple about an overhead projector which, when you are seeking interactivity, also allows you to keep looking forwards.

Creating an atmosphere

Have a think about how you might enhance the atmosphere for your presentation by dressing the room appropriately. This is a technique

I learned when working in the drinks industry, where many brands and types of drink have highly seasonal sales patterns. The challenge for us was that we usually had to launch and promote them in a completely different season. So, faced with launching a summer drink in mid-winter, I went to a theatrical props company and hired a backdrop of a country garden on a beautiful summer's day. All it needed then was to retrieve my garden furniture from the shed and we had transformed the mood to one that would enhance rather than clash with our new product.

On another occasion we had one end of the board room table set up as if for a dinner party. When the time came to discuss a promotional idea for an after-dinner drinks brand in restaurants, we dimmed the lights, lit the candles and moved to that end of the table. It was very simple to set up and had so much more impact than asking the audience to imagine they were out to dinner.

There may even be an opportunity to let the venue itself do the talking. In the early 1990s I had the task of launching a new vintage for my port wine client. A key objective was to attract younger buyers and to dispel the image that vintage port was drunk primarily by old men in their gentleman's clubs. The venue we chose, therefore, was The Groucho Club, which was then the hot new venue for London's media community. It was still a club, still had plenty of associations with eating, drinking and conviviality, but it was the very opposite of the traditional gentleman's clubs across town in Pall Mall. Just announcing The Groucho Club as the venue was a strong positioning statement in itself that would really help to underpin our messages about bringing fresh thinking to the category. On a practical note, a number of the younger, up-and-coming wine writers actually turned up to our launch. Usually they shunned such events because the Pall Mall locations chosen as venues would not allow them in without a tie.

Mock-ups to bring your idea alive

If you are presenting an idea or concept that has yet to be developed, be sure to make a mock-up. This means your ideas can be seen and felt; they almost seem real already and go way beyond a mere figment of the imagination. Trevor Bayliss, the inventor of the wind-up radio, said: "If a picture is worth a thousand words, a prototype is worth a million."

I proved this on one occasion in particular when a client had expressed his frustration at failing to forge a strong link in product terms between his beer brand and the All Blacks rugby team for which he was providing expensive sponsorship. This was some years before many brands climbed on the bandwagon of producing limited editions, so my idea for a limited edition of (all) black beer bottles was going to be a novel one. I believed it to be such a strong idea that I wanted it to come across with maximum impact, so I mocked-up some beer bottles – simply by removing the labels, taping over the caps, spraying the bottle black and re-applying the label.

When I produced an "All Black" bottle – just one to begin with – from under the table there was a look of sheer delight and excitement on the faces of the client and his colleagues, all of whom were itching to get their hands on the bottle; all the more reason to hold back the additional bottles I had under the table. It was so much more powerful than simply talking about the concept or displaying a sketch. Another reason to hold back on the additional bottles was that there was a kicker still to come. I had changed the bottle's back label to a variety of mocked-up labels, each featuring a cartoon of a different All Blacks player. Not only was this a limited edition that brought the brand and its sponsored team directly together, but there was a set of at least 15 different bottles to collect. I discuss kickers in more detail in Chapter 3.5. It is a technique that is popular with magicians, whereby you reach a climax, only for the audience to find subsequently there is another climax that either trumps the previous, apparent climax, or adds a special enhancement to it.

Finally, it is important to understand that prototypes do not have to be highly finished. They should actually be a bit rough and ready, as if they were crying out: "Come and change me. Don't leave me like this!" And even if it is a mere concept that doesn't take on a physical form, give it a name. Again, this breathes life into the idea and makes it feel like it is almost real and ready to go.

Mixed media

The best option of all – and the one most in tune with the ethos of "whatever it takes to help tell the story" – is to mix up your media. As long as it all hangs together as a cohesive whole, mixing your media ensures you have the most suitable tool for each job, plus it introduces the movement and change that are so important to retaining attention (Rule 11).

Just as producing the occasional live prop can have more impact than simply throwing another image on the screen, video clips can be great for impact and pacing. The proviso is that the clips need to be short, flexible in length and easy to switch in and out of from a technical point of view. If your clips fail in any of these respects they can easily be more of a hindrance than a help.

Always think about interactivity, considering where there are fruitful, non-invasive opportunities to get your audience involved so as to make them feel fully engaged. How could you use that flipchart or overhead projector – maybe just briefly to bring a change of tone and introduce some audience involvement?

The iPad

Finally, I cannot conclude without mention of the device that has been the big talking point during the writing of this book – the iPad or tablet computer. At the time of writing it is still too early to assess its potential as a presentation tool as people are still using it mainly for showing off and as a plaything. I suspect, however, that the iPad will prove just a little too small to be truly effective as a presentation device – bear in mind what I have just said about the frustration of an aid that can't quite be seen.

I do, however, see a couple of useful roles for the iPad and similar devices. The first is where you want to throw in an apparently impromptu idea that in fact you have thought out carefully in advance. This falls under the category of White Cheating that you will find in the Appendix; the general concept is that an idea may carry more weight if it appears to have been thought of on the spot, apparently triggered by something your audience members have said, so they feel a sense of ownership for that idea. It follows that you would not have such an idea mapped out as part of your main presentation but you might have some supporting visuals ready to hand – on your iPad.

Second, my friends Richard Hall and Martin Conradi run Showcase, a specialist presentation company that creates the most beautiful PowerPoint (yes those two words *can* go together) presentations you will ever see. Conscious that their clients are not always equipped with computers and projectors, they also produce scaled-down variants, in particular what they call "lunch books". These do exactly what they say – enable you to use a version of your beautifully produced presentation, but discretely at a lunch table. I believe iPads have the potential to fulfill a similar function, in a more hi-tech manner than a print version. The trouble is that the more brash iPad owners will spoil it for everyone else by over-using their machines in public places, so tainting the concept of using them in smarter establishments.

In a nutshell

Get deep into the minds of your audience before deciding what you are going to tell them or choosing the tools with which to deliver your communication.

Chapter 3
ATTENTION

The power of focus – clarity of objectives and what you most want your audience to remember; firsts and lasts; gaining attention; retaining attention; creating, planning and managing your climax

3.1 The power of focus

THE MOST SUCCESSFUL MAGICIANS HAVE THE SIMPLEST, CLEAREST OBJECTIVES — SAWING A WOMAN IN HALF; VANISHING THE STATUE OF LIBERTY; FLYING. THEY CAN BE SUMMED UP IN A SHORT SENTENCE, REMEMBERED AND TALKED ABOUT AFTER THE SHOW.

Rule 5 – Concentrated attention requires a Single Point of Focus

A Single Point of Focus from a physical point of view is crucial to the magician's craft in that attention must be in the right place at the right time for magic to be created; we shall look at how to create high physical focus when we come to *Delivery* in Part III. At the *Construction* stage it is even more important to create high focus from a *mental* point of view.

The starting point is your objective, which you need to define in precise terms. Is your objective to: Pass on vital information? Inspire your audience to take immediate action? Persuade in the longer term? Entertain? Something else? A hidden objective? A mixture of these?

All too often you see people embark on a presentation without really considering what they want their audience to actually do or think as a result of their presentation. Many presentations that I see are well delivered and rich in information, but ultimately of little use because they lack a definite objective. If you are clear about your objective you have a measure against which to assess achievements, and that objective will also steer you as you progress through the construction process. As we shall see, you need to be ruthless in your editing – with a clear objective, what stays in comes down to the simple question: does it move me further towards achieving my objective?

Closely allied to your objective is the big question:

What do you most want them to go away remembering? Key to this is:

> **Rule 4** – The brain filters out most information it receives, leaving only what it considers important

If you tell people a complete a list of things, they may not remember any of them; tell them one big thing, however, and they are much more likely to remember it – because you have given them a single point on which to focus. It's much better to have one thing remembered than a complete list forgotten.

So you need to create a Single Point of Focus mentally – ideally you want one big point around which to build and pace the presentation and create supporting aids.

Focusing on one big point requires great self discipline – everyone will want to force in a mention of their own particular area of interest. It is also a great challenge – most things are complicated, multi-faceted and difficult to boil down to a single message. I have spent many years specializing in re-configuring complicated messages into neat little nutshell versions and I still find it difficult, so you might like to read the section in the Appendix on Message Distillation where I take inspiration from the movie makers in creating "elevator" messages.

The trick is to aim for a Single Simple Message (SSM) that has three important properties:

1. It is simple.
2. It is distinctive.
3. It acts as a trigger to much greater detail.

One of the very best examples of a presentation based around a Single Simple Message (SSM) was Apple's launch of the MacBook Air. By their very nature computers are complicated, multi-faceted and wrapped up in technical terminology, but Steve Jobs' presentation focused on one big point – his new product was "The world's thinnest notebook." Having made the announcement: "What is it? In a sentence – the world's thinnest notebook," thinness was central to every aspect that Jobs talked about and to all the visual aids.

This example was highly distinctive and simple but it also fulfilled the third requirement of acting as a trigger to much greater detail. It paved the way for discussion of technological advances in chips, memory, and so on, and the competitive advantage they offered. All of this came over with much greater impact thanks to the context of thinness. And thanks to the simplicity of the message, it created a talking point and a resulting "need to see" the product.

Having identified your SSM you need to build and pace your presentation around that single point. If you look at the Steve Jobs presentation – and this and many others are easy to find on iTunes or YouTube – you will see that "the world's thinnest notebook" is enunciated very clearly and repeatedly by Jobs and displayed on the screen; the very simple screen graphics are all about thinness; the Air and its competitors are each described as "*X*mm thin" (rather than "thick"); the product is revealed from within a manila envelope (which subsequently features in the advertising); and Jobs displays the Air very clearly and carefully in front of his uniform black top so as to accentuate its slender proportions.

Notice also how Jobs cleverly deploys Rule 19 (*People put more reliance on something they have worked out for themselves*). By using a manila envelope you don't even need to check for yourself how thin the Air really is; you work it out for yourself and marvel at your discovery.

3.2 Firsts and lasts

WHEN WAYNE DOBSON, THE MAGICIAN WHO ENJOYED MAJOR TV AND LAS VEGAS SUCCESS IN THE 1980S, LECTURES AT THE MAGIC CIRCLE HE FOCUSES ON WHAT HAS FOR MANY YEARS BEEN HIS OPENING TRICK. HE TELLS US HOW TO PERFORM THE TRICK, BUT MORE IMPORTANTLY HE TELLS US *WHY* HE PERFORMS IT AND WHY HE PERFORMS IT *FIRST*. "I WANT TO GET THEM TO LIKE ME," HE SAYS, "AND ONCE THEY LIKE ME I KNOW I'VE GOT THEM FOR THE REST OF THE SHOW."

Having focused around a main objective and what you most want your audience to remember, you can start to plan a structure for your presentation.

The traditional view is that attention must rise progressively throughout the presentation reaching a crescendo at the end. This would actually be somewhat exhausting for both presenter and audience, so the more realistic approach is aim for a "billow" curve whereby attention rises, then lets off a little, rises again, relaxes a touch and eventually reaches the big climax. Traditional magic acts were built around a billow curve – starting with a small trick, relaxing for a moment, following with a slightly bigger trick, building to the biggest trick at the end. There might also be a fade-out at the very end, where the magician brings attention back to himself personally before finally saying good night.

This is the sort of thing that is espoused by established writers on magical theory, such as Henning Nelms, but it's all rather old-fashioned thinking. The emerging modern view is that if you hook them at the start you should sail through and you can do more or less what you want. If, on the other hand, you get off to a poor start you will be playing catch-up all the way through and you will have little chance of making your climax as big as it could be.

This is all about:

Rule 13 – Firsts and lasts are remembered

Magicians such as Wayne Dobson aside, rock bands are very familiar with Rule 13, some of them quite cynically so. They know that as long as they come on with a big number and go out with their greatest hit, they can get away with murder in the middle – such as playing the whole of their new album – and yet people still come away with good memories.

You therefore need to work on your Intro and what I call the "Outro" more than anything else. These are the elements that are going to be best remembered, so as well as rehearsing them extensively, you need to construct them with great care and in fine detail.

3.3 Gaining attention

IF YOU HAVE EVER WORRIED ABOUT HOW TO GAIN ATTENTION AT THE BEGINNING OF YOUR PRESENTATION, IMAGINE HAVING TO DO IT UNDER THE FOLLOWING CONDITIONS: AGAINST A VERY NOISY BACKGROUND; WHEN THE AUDIENCE IS NOT EXPECTING YOU; WHEN THEY ARE ENGROSSED IN CONVERSATION; IN THE MIDDLE OF A MEAL; COMPETING FOR ATTENTION WITH WAITERS; IN SEMI-DARKNESS. IF YOU SUCCEED, YOU THEN NEED TO DO IT ALL OVER AGAIN EVERY 10 MINUTES OR SO. THESE ARE THE SORTS OF CONDITIONS MAGICIANS FACE ON THE BANQUETING

CIRCUIT THAT PROVIDES ONE OF THEIR FEW SOURCES OF REASONABLY REGULAR INCOME. ACCORDINGLY, THEY HAVE ALL KINDS OF STRATEGIES FOR GAINING ATTENTION, RANGING FROM THE CRUDE (BASED AROUND SUPPOSEDLY LOST PEN KNIVES, IF YOU CAN BELIEVE IT) TO THE PSYCHOLOGICALLY SOPHISTICATED.

The old maxim of "Tell them what you are going to say, tell them and then tell them again" holds true. You certainly need to state your objective – the reason you want your audience to listen – upfront. But to do that with impact you need to *break their pattern* and surprise them a little.

Breaking the audience's "pattern"

The point is that they expect you to set the agenda and dole out a few pleasantries upfront. If you simply fulfill these expectations they will perceive you to be like almost every other presenter they have ever heard and they will go into default mode of settling down, if not for a quiet snooze, then certainly into a rather relaxed state of mind – just when you really need them stimulated. So, in conjunction with setting the agenda, aim to seize their attention. There are two main ways in which you can do this:

> You can do something a bit different – say something a little outrageous or contentious; promise them something special coming up; produce an odd looking prop or visual aid that intrigues them. Really, it can be almost anything that makes them think, "Well I wasn't expecting that, this guy might be worth a listen."
>
> You can make it interactive, such as asking for a show of hands about a specific question. This can be a great way of engaging directly and quickly with the audience as you are actively seeking information from them. This brings instant

personalization and you can then use the results as a springboard for your speech.

Avoiding attention-grabber minefields

Needless to say, as well as having the potential to help you, both of these approaches can also be minefields for the speaker. If you are going for the say-or-do-something-a-bit-different approach your tactic is intended to create a deliberate jolt, but it must, nevertheless, fit with your overall theme. If it looks gratuitous it is likely to undermine or even trivialize what you are saying at a crucial moment.

I heard a story of a speaker at a financial services conference who walked on stage with a cabbage; he immediately had everyone intrigued. He then carried on as normal, making no mention of the cabbage; he must be building up to a big point involving the cabbage, everyone thought. He concluded, still without any reference to the cabbage, so when it came to questions and answers one of the first was "What is the cabbage all about?" "What cabbage?" he replied, raising a big laugh in the process. I then asked the friend telling me the story what had been the topic of the talk; "I don't know," he said, "I can't remember." The speaker had undoubtedly succeeded in terms of gaining attention, but his attention-grabber soon became a distraction and ultimately, proved to be just a meaningless prop. Proof of his failure came with my friend's failure to recollect either the name of the speaker or his topic, let alone his message.

Throwing questions out to the audience

The interactive route is arguably even more fraught with difficulties. Unless you ask the right question it could work against you rather than for you. I once saw a Californian magician performing for a family audience in the gala show at the International Magic Convention in London. As the prelude to an escape routine he said: "Now there is one magician that everyone knows, his first name is Harry, what's his second name?" As he dangled a straitjacket, waiting for the audience to respond, a small boy at the front shouted out: "Potter." Not the best way to get into your tribute to Houdini.

I watched a speaker at a business seminar open with the question: "Who here likes skiing?" No one put their hand up, so the first six slides with visuals based on skiing fell rather flat. That person was unlucky, but not as much as a brand manager I saw speaking at a conference on board a ship. She started by asking her audience to call out the names of brands they loved. "Apple, Sony, Virgin and so on" came back as the answers. "OK, now some brands you hate, please." "Yours," said a man at the back, before relating a horror story he had experienced in dealing with the very company that the woman worked for. What had been intended as a way to get her off to a good start had worked completely the other way and she was very much on the back foot thereafter.

So how do you get it right? And you absolutely must get this bit right – remember Rule 13 *Firsts and lasts are remembered.* You don't want your strategy for engaging your audience to result in alienating them from the outset.

In the case of throwing out questions, the starting point is to make it a simple show of hands. No one feels too prevailed upon simply raising their hand, so you don't run the risk of having no one coming forward with a contribution. Then go for questions that are as "bullet proof" as possible – where you can be very certain which way the answer will go and the only possible surprise is the degree to which it goes that way.

Ideally, your question should be one whereby you can work with whatever answer comes back, that is:

- If they get the answer right you say: "You're absolutely right, but what most people think is …" (they feel good).

- If they get it wrong you say: "That is what most people think but in fact the answer is ..." (they don't feel bad and are now intrigued).

If, for instance, I was about to talk about conquering nerves when speaking publicly, I could ask: "Hands up, please, anyone who gets nervous when speaking in front of a crowd?"

- I could reasonably expect a high proportion to put their hands up, especially if I had reassured them I was not going to ask them to speak now. I could then tell them not to worry about that; most people suffer from nerves, even Tony Blair continues to do so, and I am now going to discuss how you can minimize those nerves.
- If, surprisingly, only a few people put their hands up, I could express surprise, tell them how lucky they are (even Tony Blair ...) and open a discussion as to whether they had suffered from nerves earlier in their careers or in specific situations and how they may have managed to overcome those feelings.

Unusual props

With props, make sure they are meaningful to the presentation and also that you – or whoever is speaking – are fully happy and confident in using them. There is nothing worse than a prop that is used in a half-hearted manner because the speaker feels uncomfortable with it, perhaps because it jars with their personal style. So, if you have found a prop that is going to help you communicate a key point in a distinctive and memorable manner, be big and bold about it and be sure to plan and practise the logistics of getting it on stage, producing and deploying it, then getting rid of it so as to bring the focus back to yourself.

I had the cabbage story in mind when I was asked by an industry organization to do a short presentation about their awards scheme, for which I was one of the judges. It did not bode well as I was being asked to deliver a presentation that they – rather than I – had written and constructed. Furthermore, it was all on the somewhat dry topic of the dos and don'ts of submitting your awards entry. This wasn't exactly going to enhance my reputation for creating and delivering creative presentations with real impact. So I asked the organizer to pick one big point that she really wanted to get across; she suggested the point about urging entrants not to submit big books full of press cuttings, as the judges will never have time to read them and they are big and bulky to store and transport.

So when I got up to speak I put a set of kitchen scales in front of me – breaking the pattern of the audience whose expectation was that I would simply talk to a bunch of PowerPoint slides. I delivered the bulk of the material straight, keeping it as concise as possible, building to my big point, when I announced: "Finally, we have a special tool for measuring media coverage." I knew this would be welcomed by my PR practitioner audience as many are highly sensitive about such measurement, increasingly demanding that only the most sophisticated methodologies are applied. "And here it is," I said, as I repositioned my kitchen scales. My audience started to look horrified as I proceeded to weigh a series of documents bound to look like press cuttings, declaring the biggest and fattest to be the winner, without even glancing at the contents. "Only joking," I said, before asking them to imagine this same room on a hot day in August, almost full of boxes, each of which needs to be carefully examined to find winners. Then I followed with a plea to help us in the task by providing easy to read summaries and pointers to supporting materials. The use of the scales raised a laugh in the midst of a fairly dry presentation. A number of people said they liked my ploy and would be more careful about the compilation of their press cuttings. And when it came to the judging, we didn't have to wade through quite so many enormous tomes as in previous years.

Jokes – no laughing matter

We should also spare a thought here for the misguided few who still wonder whether they should start their presentation with a joke. The answer is a categorical "No". There is a multitude of reasons for this. First, there is a real art to delivering jokes effectively; it is a talent that needs to be honed and crafted through extensive experience. Second, in these days of political correctness there is an increasingly fine line between a joke being funny and it being offensive, and that depends on the make-up of the audience and the cultures within which you are working. There is also a psychological angle that has been studied by Professor Richard Wiseman, a member of The Magic Circle who is based at the UK's University of Hertfordshire. Wiseman says that the reason jokes in Christmas crackers are universally bad is that they *need* to be bad. When you tell any kind of joke, he continues, not everyone will find the joke funny, with the result that it divides the room. With the terrible "groaning" jokes that you find in crackers, however, the scenario becomes one of "everyone against the joke", so it has a bonding effect.

Experienced comedians know all too well that what works in one situation with a specific audience won't necessarily work in another. At The Magic Circle we are fortunate enough to have Noel Britten, a gifted stand-up comedian who also runs the Bizarre Bath comedy walks, among our membership. He shares with us the strategies that he and fellow comedians use to recover from the position of a joke failing to win a laugh. He explains how they use that to gauge the audience and how they then self-edit as they go in such a way as to stand the best chance of winning the audience back. All of which leaves us with a sense of awe and, typically, a determination to leave comedy to the comics.

So let's cut straight to the chase here and imagine you have decided to use a joke as your opening gambit in a presentation. You deliver the joke and no one laughs. How would you feel, having got yourself off to the worst possible start? How are you going to recover from that and deliver the real meat of your presentation?

There is certainly a role for humour, but it's best to go for lines that stand up even if people don't laugh. When, for instance, I am explaining Rule 5 about Single Point of Focus I talk about how the best magicians avoid doing card tricks at arms' length (i.e., holding them around the groin area) because attention flits between the eyes and the groin. As I hold the cards at groin level, I say, "And you don't want to focus down there anyway!" Often this gets a laugh or a titter at least; if it doesn't, that's fine – it needed to be said anyway and I simply move more quickly to the next line: "Much better to bring them up to your face – all in one frame for a Single Point of Focus." If, by the way, it *does* get a laugh, it helps me to gauge the audience, and I can be sure of winning a few laughs later on with some material that I might have left out had I not received a positive response at this stage.

Prologues

Once you become practised at the art of the engaging introduction, you might consider extending it a little into a prologue – a short section that sets the scene before you embark on your speech proper. My lectures, for instance, start with a short trick, such as predicting a telephone number from the entire phone book. I then say: "I'm not actually going to show you how to do that. It's to introduce the fact that today we are going to be talking about applying the Rules of Magic to business communication …"

What this achieves for me is several things: the audience is immediately engaged, entertained and, hopefully, impressed. It sets out some magic credentials for me, making it apparent (Rule 19) that I have some skills in this area. Just as important, it gives the audience the opportunity to tune-in to me, look me up and down, and let first impressions sink in. So by the time I come to say anything important they are fully primed to take in what I have to say.

3.4   Retaining attention

MICHAEL VINCENT IS A MEMBER OF THE INNER MAGIC CIRCLE AND ONE OF THE WORLD'S MOST ACCOMPLISHED CARD MAGICIANS. WHEN A CARD MAGICIAN IS REQUIRED, MICHAEL IS A FIRST PORT OF CALL FOR AGENTS, BOOKERS, LECTURE ORGANIZERS, TV PRODUCERS AND MAGIC SUPPLIERS. WHEN YOU HIRE HIM TO ENTERTAIN YOU, HOWEVER, HIS BRILLIANT CARD MAGIC IS INTERSPERSED WITH CUPS AND BALLS, COINS, IMPOSSIBLE TRANSPOSITIONS OF EVERYDAY OBJECTS AND BANK NOTES THAT CHANGE DENOMINATION. AND IT'S ALL LINKED TOGETHER BY ENCHANTING STORIES. HOW EVER BRILLIANT HE IS WITH THE CARDS, HE KNOWS THROUGH MANY YEARS EXPERIENCE THAT HE NEEDS VARIATION TO HOLD THE AUDIENCE'S ATTENTION TO BEST EFFECT.

Once you have gained attention, you need to retain it and you do that by shortening mental time – using movement and change and dividing it into small chunks, so that there is always an end in sight.

Rule 11 – Attention is sustained by variation, which shortens mental time

Magicians strive for movement, change and clear chunking, but the principle can also be seen closer to home. In recent years the wonderful crime novelist Peter James has become a good friend. His bestselling books, such as *Dead Simple* and *Dead Like You*, often have around 125 chapters and as I read them I have a great feeling of pace – I am continually reaching the end of a chapter. There is another chapter about to start, but I feel I am making great progress. Similarly, TV news programmes never go for very long without some kind of change such as: "Now over to our political correspondent outside Number 10." That correspondent could often do the job just as well – better even – sitting next to the anchorman in the studio, but the movement, change and accompanying adjustments to vocal tone all help to keep our attention.

The Power of 3

When "chunking" your content you can benefit from the "Power of 3". Life is governed by threes – we have the three bears, three wishes and the Holy Trinity. Think of great speeches such as "Government of the people, by the people, for the people."

There is something about the rhythm of threes that means information in two parts leaves us anticipating a third; equally, information in four parts feels like overload. When researching this principle I realized that this is why, in the days when we told politically incorrect jokes about the Englishman, the Irishman and the Scotsman, we left out the Welsh guy. There was no reason for this other than, had we been saying, "There was an Englishman, an Irishman, a Scotsman and a Welshman," it would have lacked essential rhythm and felt like too much information.

So divide your content into threes – or sixes and nines if necessary – and it will flow all the more effectively with resultant impact. President Barak Obama is known to be an admirer of President Kennedy's speeches and many of those were written by Ted Sorenson, a great believer in the Power of 3. When Obama took the oath of office his speech included the following examples:

> I stand here today humbled by the task before us, grateful for the trust you have bestowed, mindful of the sacrifices borne by our ancestors.

> Homes have been lost, jobs shed, businesses shattered.

> Today, I say to you that the challenges we face are real, they are serious, and they are many.

3.5 Creating, planning and managing your climax

THERE IS RATHER MORE TO CREATING MAGIC THAN SIMPLY THE "TA-DAH" MOMENT AT THE END, BUT IT HAS TO BE SAID THAT MAKING THAT MOMENT SPECIAL IS CRUCIAL TO THE SUCCESS OF ANY TRICK AND IT WILL BE THIS THAT THE AUDIENCE REMEMBERS AND TALKS ABOUT AFTERWARDS.

Bearing in mind that *Firsts and lasts are remembered* (Rule 13), your climax – and it must be a climax, not just an end, if it is to have impact – needs careful planning. Clearly, *Delivery* will be essential to ensuring an effective climax but it needs planning at this *Construction* stage, with three elements:

1. **Signpost your ending** – something simple along the lines of: "As I draw to a close …" This will wake up your audience or at least re-focus their attention at a key moment.

2. **Distil your key messages,** including a call to action – what you want them to actually do or think as a result of your presentation. See the *Message Distillation* section in the Appendix.

3. **An applause cue.** Ensure that the end is definite and doesn't trail off or culminate in a muttered "That's all I have." You need to create an applause cue – something that makes it absolutely clear your conclusion has been reached. Ideally this should be self-apparent – underpinned by rising to a crescendo with your voice – but it could be as simple as "Ladies and gentlemen, *thank you* for your attention." Clearly you don't often expect to receive actual applause in a business situation, but you still need that applause cue. If you are asked, "Is that all?" you have failed. There is one other element to factor in and that is the Question

and Answer session that will probably be expected as part of your presentation. These are notoriously difficult from various perspectives to control, so I cover the handling of Q&As and, in particular, their placement, in the *Delivery* section in Chapter 14.4.

Maintaining control

Careful planning of your climax gives you the greatest chance of maintaining control over what is one of the two most important parts of your presentation (Rule 13 – *Firsts and Lasts*). With the success of a trick often dependent on the successful execution of its ta-dah moment, magicians are acutely aware of this need to maintain particular control over their climax. If, for instance, the climax of a trick depends on revealing a playing card that has been displayed face down, magicians will hesitate to let a volunteer do that for them. The volunteer may just pick up the card lamely, mumble quietly, "Yes, that's the right card," and fail to display it properly. What you need in order to create a good climax is energy, excitement, clear display with card and person in a Single Point of Focus and the timing of voice and revelation co-ordinated. That's a lot to expect from a nervous volunteer. So some of the tricks that I ask business people to present as part of their training are specifically geared to highlighting the importance of controlling your climax. I have to say that I almost want them to get it wrong the first time; then we can work on it and everyone can see how much more powerful a climax can be when kept under control. Finally, we can go back to their business presentations and discuss how the same principles can be applied in that situation.

The kicker climax

Once you have mastered the art of building to a climax you can consider the possibilities of enhancing that climax with what magicians call a "kicker" – where their audience think they have seen the big finish, but there is another, even better feature still to come.

A typical magical kicker might come in a mind reading effect where the magician has made a prediction which he puts into an envelope that is left clearly on display and never touched again until the climax. He asks for a selection of clearly random numbers, totals them up, asks for verification then opens the envelope to reveal his prediction is correct. The kicker comes when, having paused to take his applause, he inserts some slash marks between every second number in that prediction, showing that the random numbers have also added up to today's date.

Steve Jobs has a nice kicker in the launch of the MacBook Air that I discussed in Chapter 3.1. Having built his story around the line "the world's thinnest notebook", he puts up a slide of a very simple, thin oblong shape to depict the thinness of the Sony TZ series – the thinnest notebook on the market at that time. Then he overlays the size and shape of the MacBook Air, highlighting a significant improvement in thinness. Having let this message sink in and taken applause, the kicker comes when he declares: "I want to point something out here. The thickest part of the MacBook Air is still thinner that the thinnest part of the TZ series; we're talking thin here." As he says this, the graphic swings around to illustrate the point.

I would advise you to avoid getting too clever too soon with kickers and only use them if they come naturally. The pre-kicker climax has got to be strong enough in its own right to work as the main climax; only go for a kicker if you truly have something that will help to enhance it.

In a nutshell

Understand what excites the human mind and work within those limitations; then turn them to your advantage.

Chapter 4
IMPACT

*Scripting your presentation; writing for the ear
rather than the page; words for impact; the danger of
negatives; editing – learning to "kill your darlings";
visual aids; keeping a memory active*

4.1 Scripting

THE KEY TO ACHIEVING GOOD SPONTANEITY IS VERY GOOD
SCRIPTING. THE POINT OF SCRIPTING IS THAT YOU KNOW YOU
CAN GO OUT ON A DAY THAT YOU'VE GOT A TERRIBLE COLD
AND YOU'RE FEELING TERRIBLE, AND DO YOUR BEST SHOW.
AND ON A GOOD DAY YOU GO OUT AND YOU DO THAT SHOW,
AND A HUNDRED AD-LIBS OCCUR TO YOU, THEY'RE GREAT AND
THEY FORM PART OF THE SHOW THE NEXT TIME, THEY GET
ADDED TO THE SCRIPT. IT'S NOT ABOUT KILLING SPONTANEITY,
IT'S ABOUT SETTING THE FRAMEWORK AS BEST AS IT CAN BE,
TO ALLOW YOU TO HAVE THE CONFIDENCE TO MOVE INTO
OTHER AREAS.

DERREN BROWN

I hesitate to call this section "Scripting" because it tends to trigger
fears that presenters will simply recite – or even read – from a rigid
script, leaving no room for a natural approach that will help them
truly connect with their audience.

It is, however, essential to plan and plot your words in some
detail, partly because you will find that a completely natural approach
will contain many extraneous words that need discarding if the
presentation is to have impact.

I am frequently asked by friends and acquaintances for my opinion of a speech or presentation they have just given. I can often sense that they feel disappointed in themselves and my truthful answer is: "You didn't really know what you were going to say, did you?" Their response is usually along the lines of: "No, I've been so busy, I didn't really have time to rehearse and I wrote some of it on the train." Unless you get really lucky, such lack of preparation will always show.

We will come to rehearsal routines in the *Preparation* section, but if there is one simple secret to successful presentation it is this: *Know what you are going to say.* That should be blindingly obvious, but too many people fall foul of simply not being familiar enough with the words they are delivering. Part of the problem is that they see top-rated stand-up comedians who work in a long-form, conversational style – people like Billy Connolly, Eddie Izzard and Robin Williams – and it appears they are making it up as they go. In reality, if you go to see any of these people on the second, third or fourth night you will invariably find that the content is remarkably similar, right down to apparent mistakes and interruptions. If they do truly ad-lib to any extent it is: a) because they are geniuses and; b) because they have a well-defined structure around which to work. If they see the opportunity for an ad-lib they know they can risk stepping out of their planned structure because they can easily get back into it. Bear in mind also that experienced comedians often have a bank of apparent ad-libs on which to draw, so they are often on even firmer ground than you might imagine. For any kind of presenter it is the planning and plotting that goes into the structure that introduces the pacing, the points of emphasis and the subtle cues that make all the difference to the end result.

The danger to the occasional presenter is that they do not understand this reality, they fancy themselves as a bit of a joke teller and even convince themselves that an off-the-cuff approach will make their delivery all the more authentic and sincere. Worse, they may even enjoy a challenge and perhaps boast of their prowess at winging it. I reiterate: if there is one simple secret to successful presentation it is *knowing what you are going to say*. This so often lies at the root of success in terms of clarity, confidence and delivery generally. The reverse is even more true.

Finally, there is another good reason for planning very carefully what you are going to say. Many people find it very difficult knowing how and when to stop. They may have been racked with nerves about the very thought of speaking, but once they get going, they keep going, often for much longer than is necessary and it all turns into a ramble that can only then be concluded by a rather abrupt halt. Coming to a conclusion actually needs careful construction and, as we saw in Chapter 3.5, this is one of the two parts that Rule 13 (*Firsts and Lasts*) tells us your audience is going to remember most clearly.

4.2 Writing for the ear

MAGICIANS HAVE THE ADVANTAGE HERE IN THAT THEY ARE MOSTLY WRITING FOR THE EAR; FURTHERMORE, BECAUSE THEY OFTEN START A NEW PERFORMANCE EVERY FEW MINUTES THEY FIND OUT VERY QUICKLY — THROUGH THE RESPONSES THEY RECEIVE — WHICH WORDS WORK AND WHICH DON'T.

MAGICIANS ARE THEREFORE VERY AWARE OF THE SUBTLE BUT IMPORTANT DIFFERENCES BETWEEN CONVERSATION AND PRESENTATION. IN PARTICULAR, THEY DEVELOP AN ACUTE UNDERSTANDING OF THE BENEFITS OF LANGUAGE THAT IS CONCISE AND CLEAR.

There is a particular pressure to speak clearly when you are in presentation mode because, unlike when your audience is reading a book or engaged in conversation, there is little if any opportunity to go back to something they have not quite understood. The words you use should therefore be short, easy to say and easy to take in.

Saying the words out loud as you write them is the key to achieving this as it keeps your language conversational and plain-English in style. While emailing and texting have shaken up the way we use the written word, there is still a tendency to dress our language in a cloak of formality when we lay it out on a page; words such as "hereinafter" and "aforementioned" start to creep in. These are perfectly good words but you wouldn't generally use them when having a conversation, so they are going to sound stilted in a presentation.

Screenwriting legend Aaron Sorkin, who created the *West Wing*, is a great advocate of speaking out loud as you write. He says: "My writing process is physical. I stand up and talk." This may help to explain why the *West Wing* had so many scenes with the lead characters conversing while walking along corridors. Saying the words out loud also helps you identify any potential tongue twisters that might look perfectly harmless on the page but could slap you around the mouth when you come to say them out loud. I once inserted some specially tailored material into a presentation at a late stage without saying it out loud. When I came to say "incongruities" my tongue simply refused to say the word that my brain was sending it. And I shouldn't have been saying it anyway; when did I last go home and say: "I've had a really tough day, just one incongruity after another."? Another time I tripped up was the first time I ever said "Christina Aguilera" out loud; unfortunately I was speaking live on national radio at the time.

Saying your words out loud as you write them brings the additional benefit of helping to avoid unfortunate mis-pronunciations. The fact is that when you are under pressure the brain and mouth don't always synchronize in the way you would expect and slight variations may creep out. "Organism" is a classic example, and as I write one of BBC Radio 4's most seasoned presenters has been just tripped up live on air while introducing the government minister Jeremy Hunt. If you can find a substitute for difficult words you will be defusing a potential bomb.

Finally, another good reason for using language that is easy to say and easy to take in is that you want your immediate audience to be able to pass your messages on to others and to do so accurately. If you have the focused approach of an SSM (Single Simple Message) with simple language around it, you stand the best chance of success.

4.3 **Words for impact**

DARWIN ORTIZ, AN ACCLAIMED EXPERT ON MAGIC THEORY, HAS A SAYING: "AUDIENCES ARE EASILY CONFUSED, BUT NOT EASILY FOOLED." THEY WILL IMMEDIATELY SPOT AN ANOMALY AND YET APPARENTLY FAIL TO UNDERSTAND WHAT SEEMED LIKE A SIMPLE INSTRUCTION. THE POTENTIAL FOR CONFUSION TENDS TO BE EXACERBATED BY NERVES WHEN AN AUDIENCE MEMBER HAS BEEN INVITED TO HELP ON STAGE.

CLARITY AND NON-AMBIGUITY BECOME PARAMOUNT IF THE AUDIENCE IS TO UNDERSTAND THE PROCEEDINGS AND THE VOLUNTEER IS TO HELP THE MAGICIAN MAKE IT WORK.

Writing for the ear releases you from the need for perfect grammar, so start by placing the most important words at the front of sentences, for example:

• The front is the best place for the most important words.

> Lower costs and increased output – that's what we need.
> *rather than:*
> We need lower costs and increased output.

> Carbon emissions have increased by 15 per cent in the past decade – according to a new study by Greenstat International's Research Unit.

rather than:

A new study by Greenstat International's Research Unit indicates that carbon emissions have increased by 15 per cent in the past decade.

Use the pronoun "you" often. This helps to make the audience feel included, important, even the focus of your communication, because it feels directly targeted at them.

Use active verbs such as "run", "go", "push", "pull" – they will help invigorate the minds of your audience.

Similarly, Words That Paint Pictures will register much more effectively as your audience can "see" what you are saying as well as hear it. The phrase "words that paint pictures" itself conjures up images of artists, brushes and easels, whereas the alternative "visual imagery" ironically sparks no particular imagery. A good example came from a PR executive I was training; he was presenting the media coverage he had achieved for a campaign, using slides of various press cuttings and building to a climax with a piece from the *Financial Times*. Just before revealing it he said, "The next one is a piece of real 'trophy coverage'," so transforming a rather plain-looking piece of newspaper into an image laced with the exhilaration of a footballer having just won the World Cup.

Magicians deploy Words That Paint Pictures to add impact and also to overcome the audience confusion identified by Darwin Ortiz. Try asking people to hold out their hands and you will soon discover there is a surprising number of options, few of which may suit the magician at a crucial point in a trick when his own hands are full, so not free to demonstrate. By "painting a picture" with words such as: "Please hold out your hands, Oliver Twist-style," they usually get the right response first time.

Strong words add real impact, so weak words should be transformed into stronger alternatives. "Might", "hopefully", "think" and "try" are all examples of weak words and as such have no place in presentation. One marketing executive I was training declared: "I am trying to develop new products." "What do you mean trying?" I asked him and he explained that he had yet to launch any. "Never mind that," I said, "I want to hear that you are actively engaged in new product development. 'Trying' suggests that you might fail." Most words can be strengthened if a little thought is applied at the planning stage. For instance, if we have "problems" it is better to say "challenges" – we all like a challenge and people receive plaudits for taking them on. If something is "manageable" then a more positive description would be "achievable". Consider a phrase such as "I think we are going to meet our targets" and see how much stronger it is if you substitute one word: "I believe we are going to meet our targets," and stronger still: "I believe we are going to achieve our targets."

The "strong" principle also applies to the expression of quantities. For instance, rather than "at least" say "more than" or "in excess of". This was brought home to me with some force by a bunch of DJs at a radio station I was helping to launch. For more than six months prior to the launch I had been boasting about the station's super-powerful transmitter that had an output of half-a-million watts. One of the DJs called me saying they wanted to make jingles about this fact, but didn't want to be talking in halves. Interestingly, they also wanted to paint pictures in the minds of their audience, so they quizzed me about the height of the transmitter. Soon we were hearing booming DJ voices declaring: "Transmitting 500,000 watts of power from twice the height of the Eiffel Tower, this is Atlantic 252."

Strong words are one of the factors that differentiate presentation style from mere conversation. While presentation style should be essentially conversational in tone, it needs ratcheting up a notch or two, making the delivery clearer, more concise and more direct than is necessary in a simple conversation where there is interplay with another person. I discuss this concept in more detail in the Appendix.

Finally, it is worth remembering that the strength of different words shifts and changes over time. I have just suggested that "challenge" is a stronger word that "problem", but friends in the financial sector report that, the deeper we get into recession, the more people start reporting their problems as challenges, with the result that it is becoming something of a cliché.

Alliteration is frowned upon by some but can be effective and memorable if used sparingly. It has worked well for these people, so it can work for you.

> We cannot fail of falter – Winston Churchill
> *Veni, vidi, vici* – Julius Caser
> Let us go forth and lead the land we love – JF Kennedy
> Fair is foul and foul is fair – William Shakespeare

Words beginning with *k* need a mention for two reasons. The first is that we need to nail the myth put about by certain comedians who would have us believe that words beginning with *k* are funny words; they cite examples such as "kimono" and "kipper" as if to prove the point. The fact is that in the hands – or mouths – of a skilled comedian almost any word can be made funny. And let's face it, they want to control where the laughs come, not have them triggered intermittently because the route to their punchline happens to involve a few *k* words. As with most myths, however, this one is based on a grain of truth. *K* words do have a certain power, in that they force you to smile; try it for yourself and see what happens. This takes us into *Delivery* territory, but if at the *Construction* stage you find the opportunity to use some *k* words then let them flow because a smile can be heard in the voice, bringing animation to your delivery.

4.4 The danger of negatives

MAGICIANS STRIVE TO CREATE A SINGLE POINT OF FOCUS, BOTH PHYSICALLY AND IN THE MINDS OF THEIR AUDIENCE. IF THEIR INSTRUCTIONS ARE NOT COMPLETELY CLEAR THEIR VOLUNTEER COULD EASILY RUIN THEIR TRICK. USING NEGATIVES, SUCH AS "DON'T MOVE AN INCH," CREATES AT LEAST TWO POINTS OF FOCUS WHEREBY THE PERSON IS FORCED FIRST TO THINK ABOUT MOVING, THEN ABOUT NOT DOING THAT, WHILE ALSO HAVING TO CONSIDER A DEGREE OF MEASUREMENT. BY COMPARISON, THE INSTRUCTION "KEEP ABSOLUTELY STILL," GETS STRAIGHT TO THE POINT.

Negatives are interesting because they actually impede communication – they need unscrambling before they can be properly understood. Imagine for a moment that you are asking a small child to carry a large tray of drinks; you might say: "Don't drop it." In all likelihood they will drop it because the way their brains are going to take in this information is as follows: first, "drop it" – got that as the basic concept; second, "don't", by which time it is probably too late. All the emphasis has been on dropping so that is what happens. It's like saying, "Don't think of a grey elephant" – it becomes impossible to avoid thinking of a grey elephant.

Double negatives confuse the mind even further, particularly in certain parts of the world such as China. London Mayor Boris Johnson received a spoof award from the Plain English campaign for his use of the multiple negative phrase:

"I could not fail to disagree with you less."

I *think* he is saying he agrees, but you have to unscramble and unscramble to get through to the actual meaning.

Johnson does, however, provide a clue to the roots of this particular problem in that, as an Old Etonian, he is typical of the upper-middle-class Englishmen who can't quite bring themselves to say what they actually mean. Phrases such as: "I spent a not inconsiderable amount of time last night with a couple of not unattractive women" come forth from uptight Englishmen, as if it were impolite to be any more specific. Various cultures have a tendency to talk around certain subjects, but I suspect that superfluous negatives come down largely to old-fashioned British reserve.

The solution to eliminating negatives is to transform them into positives wherever possible; this is all the more effective because we think in positives and pictures:

> *"Don't drop it" (that tray of drinks)*
> – "Hold it steady."
> There is a certain amount you can actually *do* about the latter instruction, but nothing except think negatively about the former.

> *Cheques are not accepted without a guarantee card.*
> – We are happy to accept cheques supported by a guarantee card.

> *Viewing strictly by appointment only.*
> – for details of this exciting opportunity contact ...

Exceptions
There are of course exceptions to the avoid negatives rule.

* First, in certain situations you can use antithesis effectively to reverse a way of thinking, for example: JF Kennedy's "Ask not what your country can do for you, but what you can do for your country."

- Second, you can sometimes use a negative to plant an idea in an objective and credible manner, for example: "Don't buy it unless you are absolutely sure of …"
- Third, sometimes a negative is the least cumbersome way to say what you mean. If you look back to the start of this section you will see that I have used a mild negative – "unscramble" – in the explanation. This is because it was the most direct way of saying what I meant. Indeed, some negatives have become so firmly embedded in our language that their negative connotations have been largely lost and they become the favoured option. "Unforgettable", for instance, is arguably more powerful than "memorable" even though the former is made up mostly of the very thing we are seeking to avoid.

It's back to school for the best example I have ever seen of the avoid negatives principle and it qualifies as the best example because I witnessed its impact immediately and very directly. My son's half-term report arrived and concluded with the following assessment:

> He is making every effort to be efficient and well organized, not without success.

The report was positive throughout, but my boy was in tears – he saw "not success" and "without success", his little 11-year-old brain not stopping, or being able, to unscramble the message. What the teacher was really saying, of course, was *with success*.

4.5 Editing

As part of their quest to direct attention exactly where they want it, the best magicians live by the maxim "If it doesn't add, it detracts." So they are ruthless in editing down their performance to the bare essentials.

Having honed your words, seemingly close to perfection, you now have to face the agonizing prospect of throwing some – maybe even many – of them away.

For true clarity you need to eliminate anything that doesn't actively help to make the point. Magicians, whose business is all about directing attention exactly where they want, usually to maximize the effect of a big finish, are acutely aware of this principle.

This is difficult to do because the content that potentially needs to be thrown out may be very personal to you, as well as carefully crafted. Little wonder, then, that film makers refer to the process as "killing your darlings". They have gone to all the trouble of writing dialogue, creating a set, performing and filming, only for their precious creation to end up on the cutting room floor. It is useful and educational to watch the deleted scenes sections that you find within the extras on DVDs. TV shows on DVD have a particular pertinence as they have to fit their content into very specific time allocations and build in breaks for advertising. Switch on the director's commentary for these deleted scenes and you will hear comments such as: "This is a beautiful piece of dialogue, nicely delivered by both the lead players, but it wasn't really moving the story forward, so it had to go." There is a useful lesson there; if in doubt about a specific element of your content, consider: "Is it really moving the story forward?"

Bear in mind that we all tend naturally to pad our speech with a lot of extraneous and unnecessary words. This is acceptable in casual conversation because we need the thinking time that they facilitate, but it soon becomes irritating in presentation. This is part of the reason for preparing properly and understanding that you are never going to make a really good presentation straight off the cuff. Make a point of listening to people speaking in formal or semi-formal situations and think how it could be tightened up by deleting much of the language and substituting some phrases with simpler, more direct alternatives. Also, thinking back to the power of focus, bear in mind that some of the most memorable and enduring pieces of communication are surprisingly short. The Lord's Prayer has a mere 71 words; The Ten Commandments extend to just 297 words; and the Gettysburg Address was all wrapped up in 271.

Final edit to ensure you are triggering the right perceptions

A final task when editing is to do all you can – having earlier assessed the perceptions and associations you are triggering – to check that you are not inadvertently triggering unsuitable or unhelpful perceptions. To give you an example, I used to talk about a particular TV programme in my training, referring to it as the "second most complained about programme ever shown on Channel 4". My intention was to underline the fact that the programme had received a huge amount of complaints; ideally I wanted to conjure images of furious people, jammed switchboards and reprimands. What actually happened was that it prompted a completely different thought in the minds of my audience: what was the *number one* most complained about programme? Worse still, it sparked a debate, and what was meant to enhance my point was undermining it in a big way. So be absolutely sure you are opening the right "files" in the minds of your audience – beware triggering red herrings.

4.6 **Visual aids**

AS THE MASTERS OF DIRECTING ATTENTION, MAGICIANS ARE PARTICULARLY WELL ATTUNED TO THE POWER OF COLOUR, EVOCATIVE PATTERNS AND ANYTHING THAT HELPS TO CATCH THE EYE. THEY KNOW WHEN TO USE VISUAL DEVICES TO THEIR ADVANTAGE BUT ALSO WHEN TO HOLD BACK LEST THE VISUALS ACT AS A DISTRACTION. IN RECENT YEARS MAGIC HAS SEEN A LESS-IS-MORE APPROACH COMING TO THE FORE; SOMETIMES – SUCH AS WITH STREET MAGIC AND CLOSE-UP MAGIC – VISUAL PROPS GET IN THE WAY AND DIMINISH THE POWER OF THE PERFORMER.

In the introduction to PowerPoint in Chapter 2.6, I touched on statistics that indicate the power of visual content in both communicating information and ensuring it is remembered. People think in positives and in pictures, so if you tell them something, they need to convert that into a picture in their mind. By showing them a picture, you can short-circuit the process for them.

I am sometimes asked: "If the visual sense is so important to taking in and retaining information, is it better to use pictures rather than words?" The short answer is that you should use whatever technique best conveys your message.

The practical answer is to write your presentation in words and then consider:

- Do my words beg a visual question? I have often heard presenters give effusive descriptions of how beautiful something looks. Well in that case, show us a picture and we can work that out for ourselves (Rule 19) much more quickly than it takes for you to tell us. Other presenters start describing a location and get themselves in a bit of a tangle. By showing us a simple map that information could be conveyed much more quickly and effectively.
- Could my words benefit from some clarification? Imagine you are recommending that your audience work with a variety of different TV personalities. If you simply mention the names and perhaps describe their personalities, some of the audience may have only a vague idea of who those personalities are or they may confuse one name with another. If, however, you show pictures, all becomes clear *and* it brightens up the slide.
- Could I use pictures to convey a lot of detail very quickly and effectively? The classic example here is a company revealing the names of its clients. Reading a list can take time if you have a lot of clients and displaying a list makes for a dull, word-filled slide. Displaying a slide full of logos, however, makes a much brighter

slide and the audience's attention will be drawn to the logos that are most meaningful and attractive to them. A wise presenter will draw specific attention to just a few of the logos, ideally responding to interest shown, while the full range and extent of clients remains on show.

- If you are using a simile or metaphor you are doing so in order to create more vivid images in the minds of your audience. So consider how you can add even more impact by illustrating those similes and metaphors, possibly letting a theme evolve as you progress. By way of example I use the theme of *Devils and Angels* when coaching people about the Seven Deadly Sins of PowerPoint. This highlights stark differences between good and bad practice and provides the potential to develop the images in such a way that "good" eventually succeeds over "evil".

- Finally, could I simply brighten up my presentation materials with some visuals? The trick here is to give them a lift without inadvertently creating distractions. Also, you don't want to be too literal or use pictures just for the sake of it; sometimes Words That Paint Pictures (see Chapter 4.3) can stimulate the senses more effectively. I once saw two different presenters speak on a holiday theme, and they each wanted the audience to sense the feeling of being on a beautiful beach. The first presenter simply put up a picture. The second asked us to close our eyes while he talked of the sights and sounds that would surround us in such a location. The second presenter was by far the more successful in achieving his objectives.

When to avoid visual aids

There are certain situations in which you should actually be wary of using visuals. I have just discussed the need to be ruthless in editing and how you need to face up to "killing your darlings". The same principle – *if it doesn't actively add to what you are saying, it will detract* – applies to visual aids. The problem is that we find a particular picture, we like it and we want to use it. We may well need to kill some "darling" visual aids as well as "darling" stories.

The acid test of whether a visual is actually helping to convey your information is to try it out on a third party; you might even find that the aid is creating confusion rather than adding clarification. I was working with another trainer for a three-day course and he tipped me off to the fact that he had some rather dry information to deliver on the topic of identity and how the law relating to it was changing. So he decided to brighten it all up by showing a picture of Tom Cruise from a film in which he has his identity stolen. I wasn't convinced this was going to help and, sure enough, when he put up the Tom Cruise slide no one had seen the film. So he had to describe the plot of the film, taking him quite a long way from what he really wanted to say. His aid was distracting rather than adding. Then one person thought they *had* seen the film, but he had to say: "No that was a different Tom Cruise film in which …" By now his aid had led the audience completely away from the topic it was meant to illustrate.

Bear in mind that some things simply cannot be readily summed up in a single visual image. And this is not a situation in which to relish a challenge; you cannot afford any ambiguity. I was coaching the head of a media monitoring agency who was about to deliver a presentation with the central message "The audience has taken control of the media." Now, that concept is probably impossible to convey in a picture, but he was determined to find a visual solution. What he came up with was a big missile swirling around in the air in circles. "That," I said "does not say 'the audience has taken control', it says 'out of control'. What's more, it is too aggressive as an image – it will spark a range of unhelpful perceptions and associations." We never did find a suitable alternative, but agreed that we needed to think more along the lines of pictures of audience members sitting in editors' chairs. Though exactly what an editor's chair looks like presents another conundrum.

Three final points on visuals:

1. Do make sure that any visual aid you use is scaled to suit the size of the audience. There is nothing worse than a visual aid that can't quite be seen. Conversely, if your visual aids are too big to hold easily you need to think carefully about two things. Ask why are they so big? Is it because you have a large audience? If so, might they work better as a projected image on a screen? Is it because they need to convey a large amount of information? If so, might they work better broken up into a series of smaller elements? Second, how you are going to manage them physically – getting them to the venue, keeping them prior to the reveal, and putting them away subsequently.

    Most of all, how are you going to keep your aids in position as you present? I once saw an excellent presentation from the editorial director of a leading publishing house and for a very plausible reason he had a very large board as the centerpiece of his presentation. He presented very well prior to the reveal of the board; he presented quite well as he talked through the board, but not as effectively as he had earlier. The reason for the deterioration in his performance was very clear – he was clinging to the board, fearful that it would collapse onto the meeting room table. As a result, he was less focused and a little distracted, and his gestures and movement generally were severely constricted. I suggested he made a simple flap to go on the back of the board – then his visual aid would be supporting him, rather than him supporting it!

2. A valuable lesson about thickness of line that I learned direct from Ali Bongo, who was President of The Magic Circle until his death in 2009. "Thickness of line is more important to visibility than

sheer scale," were the words of wisdom he shared with us one night at The Magic Circle. This was in response to a member who was showing us small boards with words written on them, that he used for his mind reading act in clubs. He was about to embark on a theatre tour as a support act to a big name, so he said he was planning to have the word boards blown up much bigger to suit the bigger audiences. "Don't do that," said Ali, "they will be expensive, difficult to handle and hardly any more effective. Keep them the same size but use a thicker font or a fatter felt pen and they will be visible to the whole theatre. Thickness of line is more important to visibility than sheer scale."

3. Avoid giving your visual aids a caption unless there is a pressing need. As you present you can *say* what might appear in a caption if it feels necessary. Furthermore, the lack of a caption enables flexibility – you have the potential to put that visual aid to different uses or even change the "spoken caption" you had planned, according to the mood of the meeting.

4.7   Keeping a memory active

WHY IS IT THAT TOMMY COOPER IS WIDELY REMEMBERED, RESPECTED AND LOVED MORE THAN 25 YEARS AFTER HIS DEATH, AND YET TOMMY WONDER, ONE OF THE MOST TALENTED AND CREATIVE MAGICIANS OF HIS GENERATION, NEVER EVEN BECAME TRULY FAMOUS? THERE IS A VARIETY OF REASONS, BUT THE CERTAIN MATTER OF A FEZ IS PROMINENT AMONG THEM.

To be sure of having anything remembered you need a degree of repetition.

Rule 16 – Sustained impact depends on transferring information to long-term memory

Short-term memory can only handle around seven items, such as names, letters and words, at once, and repetition helps to transfer them to long-term memory. To be effective, repetition needs a stealthy approach – if you simply keep repeating the same thing your audience may remember it, but with an increasing degree of irritation. So you need to find ways to weave the repeat messages seamlessly into your script, possibly as a summarizing line every time you conclude a set of points.

Once again, Apple's CEO Steve Jobs is the master of effective repetition. Watch a presentation such as the MacBook Air launch and that SSM "The world's thinnest notebook" crops up at the opening and close of every section of his beautifully chunked-up delivery. He uses the repeated line both as a pacing device and to create a sense of celebration.

The most stealthy approach of all is to combine a degree of well-placed repetition with two techniques I have already discussed: *Building on what your audience already knows* (Rule 3) with plenty of familiar reference points; and *personalizing* the message to your audience, so as to overcome the brain's filtering process (Rule 4). Apply these principles, and repetition becomes almost redundant.

Differentiation devices

To keep a memory active, you need to go a little further and fix it in the audience's minds. This usually requires a device of some kind and that device can often be something extremely simple. With Steve Jobs, for instance, the line "World's thinnest notebook" created high focus, but arguably it was the *device* of the envelope from which he removed the MacBook Air that truly fixed it in our minds. That device was, of course, then seen repeatedly throughout the advertising campaign that followed.

As I say, the device can often be very simple – as simple as an envelope. We are talking about differentiation – something that helps you to stand out from the crowd and fix the memory, with relevant associations, in the minds of your audience. We are talking about Rule 15 – *Over-familiarity leads to "invisibility"*.

The need for differentiation becomes acute when you are in a pitch situation – competing for a specific piece of business alongside a number of competitors. In the latter days of my PR career, I did some work advising clients on their choice of PR consultancy and as a starting point I recommended they visit several contenders in their own offices. That way my clients could get a feel for the people and culture at different consultancies before inviting a small selection to visit their own office to make a pitch. My clients dutifully came to town and visited the consultancies on my list and I then called the next day to hear their initial reactions. What invariably happened was that they remembered one person and one fact from each place they had visited and then got everything else muddled up. The reason for this was that, realistically, there was little to differentiate one offering from another. Had one of the consultancies employed a simple device to fix themselves in the mind of their potential new client they could have been ahead of the game.

In my PR days I ensured visitors to my consultancy firm had at least a couple of very clear memories fixed in their minds. Not every business can have an office that looks out onto the Tower of London, as mine did, but they can all have a conversation piece in their lobby or boardroom. Among other items, I had a life-size representation of Elton John that I had acquired at the Christie's auction of Elton's belongings. Visitors went away with a clear memory of "the PR company with Elton John in their boardroom"; and if they didn't like that, we were probably the wrong PR company for them.

To steer my trainees in the right direction with regard to differentiators, I tell them the story of Michael Grade, who was famous in the UK as a high-ranking TV executive, but was little known in the USA where he subsequently went to work. He soon realized he was going to have to do something to stamp his identity on the American entertainment world. His British accent helped in setting himself apart, but the clincher was again very simple – he took to wearing red socks. At the time this was considered by the Americans to be a rather eccentric British trait, so it fixed him in their minds. He would call people up, identify himself and they would say: "O yeah, I remember you, you're the guy with the red socks." Job done.

My own differentiator these days – aside from building magic into my training – is a device I use when I am visiting people to prospect for business. I wanted to use some visual aids but I was determined not to be another person turning up with a laptop, so I created an alternative. When they invite me to describe my offering I respond by saying: "Much of my work revolves around the flipchart. So when I am talking with just one or two people I use a miniature flipchart." From my case I then produce what looks exactly like a standard flipchart – complete with Nobo branding – except that it is scaled down to take A4-sized paper. Almost always I get a great reaction to this, especially from women. They ask where I got it, how they can get one and so on – it is a conversation piece. On occasions that I return for a second meeting I have even had people say: "I've heard about your flipchart." They are remembering me and even talking about me – because of a simple little device.

In a nutshell

Presenters have a whole smorgasbord of ingredients with which they can spice up their offering, but these will only be effective if they have paid proper care and attention to the basic recipe.

Chapter 5
CONVICTION

Self-conviction; being yourself; openness –
and accidental convincers; un-convincers;
beware auto-pilot; self-confidence

"ONLY HE WHO IS CONVINCED CONVINCES."

MAX DESSOIR, FRENCH PSYCHOLOGIST
(ADVISED MAGICIANS IN THE LATE 19TH CENTURY)

When it comes to *Conviction*, it is clear that a lot will depend on how you come across in *Delivery*. However, you need to consider the essential building blocks for *Conviction* during the *Construction* process.

5.1 Self-conviction

Nowadays Max Dessoir would probably say something more along the lines of "You can tell a bullshitter a mile off." Or he might put it rather more elegantly, along the lines of contemporary magician Michael Vincent, who says to fellow members of The Magic Circle: "Your fear will always betray you before your technique does." The point he makes is that you need a lot of self-belief; it is little use magicians practising all their clever sleight of hand moves to the nth degree if their face is still looking as guilty as hell.

Dessoir encouraged his trainees to build their messages around what they personally could most believe in, so that their conviction would shine through. I related to this by thinking back to my days of promoting mass-market drinks brands. Just occasionally people would tease me and ask whether I drank specific clients' brands at home. The truthful answer was no, they were rather too sweet and bland for my taste. What I felt highly confident about, however, was the widespread distribution of these brands, their award-winning advertising campaigns, huge awareness levels and formulation that was perfectly attuned to the palates of the mass market. So these were the messages on which I focused – with a large degree of true passion showing through.

5.2 **Being yourself**

The starting point to Conviction is undoubtedly being yourself; indeed, unless you are the finest actor, you can *only* be convincing if you are being yourself. So don't try and copy someone else; let your words and actions come from your own heart. You can take this principle a little further by "letting a little light in on yourself" – build in a few references to your own private life and the audience will warm to you with the result that your overall communication becomes more convincing.

The benefits of letting some light in on yourself can often be seen on my training days when the delegates learn and present a magic trick. With some people the business presentation they have given earlier in the day has been overly formal, delivered in a straight, humourless manner that they deem appropriate to delivering a business presentation. This seems to be especially prevalent when presenting to a client whose money they are responsible for. When they come to present their trick, however, their whole body language changes, there is a smile on their face which we can hear in their voice and, importantly, they are telling us things about themselves. Suddenly we are getting a small insight into the person behind the money-making machine we were hearing from earlier and we start warming to them, with the result that they come over as more convincing.

Dai Vernon, the hero of so many within the magic fraternity used to say: "If they like you as a person, they will like what you do." King of the Spanish magic world Juan Tamariz underpins this with: "If an audience likes you, they don't want to catch you out, they want you to succeed."

5.3 Openness and "accidental convincers"

As part of being yourself, work to develop a natural sense of openness.

> **Rule 18** – Doubts are reduced by openness, but may be increased by over-stressing

Magicians will take every opportunity to hand out their props for examination, offer apparently completely free choices, ask a volunteer if they want to change their mind and so on. They appear to be ceding control but are actually strengthening it because they are creating conviction.

This approach can be adopted in business with offers such as "Ask me anything you like", "Feel free to wander around", "Speak to any of our clients". By appearing so open you may win them over without the need for further action. Third-party endorsement is the obvious convincer, but you can take this principle a stage further with what magicians call the "accidental convincer".

> **Rule 19** – People put more reliance on something they have worked out for themselves

Rule 19 lies at the heart of the accidental convincer, which is all about communicating through suggestion, allowing the audience to come to their own conclusion. By way of example, if a magician drops something while on stage it may simply be that he is clumsy. It is more likely, however, that he wants to draw attention – in a natural way – to his empty hand as he retrieves the item. It is then all the more impressive when he subsequently produces something from that apparently empty hand – much more impressive than if he had made overt statements about his hand being empty. Human nature is such that your brain will believe anything that you tell it, while it will question anything that anyone else tells it.

There is a magician called James Freedman who cleverly applies this principle in the business world when selling his consultancy services. Rather than going into a meeting and reeling off the names of past clients, he finds it much more effective to do this by accidental convincer. During the meeting he will find an excuse to open his brief case, inside of which he has files with spines clearly marked with the names of famous-name clients. The people in the meeting spot this and are now convinced they are talking to a heavyweight – much more so than if he had been telling them directly.

5.4 Un-convincers

Think carefully about "un-convincers" so that you can avoid them. Rule 18 says that *doubts may be increased by over-stressing*, so watch out for protesting too much. Inexperienced magicians fall into traps such as declaring: "I have here a perfectly ordinary pack of cards," which immediately makes most people assume there's probably something dodgy about them, even if they happen to be perfectly innocent. If you want the audience to know the cards are regular and properly mixed, show them as such or ask someone to shuffle them for you. That way they work out for themselves (Rule 19) the message that those inexperienced magicians are trying too hard to deliver.

5.5 Beware switching to auto-pilot

Watch out also for switching to auto-pilot while presenting; many people do this just at the point that they need to be most convincing. By auto-pilot I mean the sort of sing-song voice that people like receptionists and airline stewards adopt because they are saying the same thing over and over again, parrot-fashion. The same thing can happen in business presentations, especially when delivering content such as company credentials that people tend to say in the same way on every occasion. If you do this it will probably *sound* as though you are simply trotting out the same old script, and that is a mistake in itself.

With company credentials think carefully about which elements your specific audience actually wants to hear. What will motivate them and encourage them to sit up and pay close attention? I once worked for a company whose chairman was rightly proud that we had offices in London, New York and Hong Kong, so every presentation started with, "We have offices in …" And yet for many of the clients we dealt with, the New York and Hong Kong offices had no relevance at all. One that I presented to found it a definite turn-off – he was looking for a consultancy with a much more local focus than we were indicating.

With one team I was training, every member used the same line at a key point in their presentation: "We are really excited about this opportunity." That's a nice, appropriate thing to say, but they each delivered it in such a mechanical and unemotional manner that it made no impact and jarred with the rest of their content. Clearly they had been told to say this line, but they should have received the further instruction to put it into their own words and find a natural place for its inclusion. It brings us back to the starting point for Conviction – you must be yourself or it will not come over as genuine. Equally, it points to an issue I shall cover in the *Delivery* section, concerning matching your body language with your words – it's no good saying you are excited if you don't look or sound excited!

5.6 Self-confidence

To conclude we return to Max Dessoir, who also used to say: "Don't position yourself below the level of your audience." He said this to magicians and it rings true with another piece of contemporary advice they receive – *Be sure to dress as well as your audience, or preferably slightly better.*

I believe this tip holds good in business as well. The point is that if you come over as too subservient you have no chance of owning the space, holding strong eye contact or deploying many of the other techniques that are so important to engaging your audience. I can think of a number of occasions in business when I have been thanked, praised and even rewarded for giving forthright advice; I don't remember anywhere I have been reprimanded for being rude or getting above my station.

Finally, a tip to help you exude a little bit of additional self-confidence: Aim to have an element in every presentation that you are actively going to *enjoy* delivering. The anticipation will pump up your energy levels and the moment itself will give you a chance to shine and truly be yourself.

In a nutshell

Communicating with conviction certainly needs a combination of sincerity and polished presentation; to be truly effective, though, it also requires planning.

Chapter 6
CONSTRUCTING A POWERPOINT PRESENTATION THAT SUPPORTS YOU AS A PRESENTER

Three underlying principles of Powerful PowerPoint;
10 progressive Construction steps

Having established the pitfalls to be avoided with PowerPoint (see Chapter 2.6), I point those I am coaching to the three essentials to achieving what I call "Powerful PowerPoint". This has very little to do with the technical operation of PowerPoint – you should work to a properly designed template and lean on administrative and IT support for that. What it *is* all about is ensuring that PowerPoint truly supports you as a presenter and steers you clear of "death-by" syndrome.

To achieve Powerful PowerPoint you need to understand three important principles:

1. **Recognize and understand those Seven Deadly Sins**. Once your eyes have been properly opened to the nature of the sins, the damage they do and how easily they can be avoided, you won't keep committing them. The most effective way to do this is to observe other people's presentations. Play Seven Sins Bingo, if you like, promising yourself a special award if you spot a Full House.

2. **Uncover the lights under PowerPoint's bushel.** There are actually a number of features and tools built in to PowerPoint specifically to help presenters. The trouble is that few people ever get to find out about them. Once you know them you will use them to enhance your delivery and probably guard them as trade secrets.

By way of example, I always ask the people I am coaching for a show of hands as to how many know what would happen if I pressed the B key while projecting a PowerPoint presentation. Typically, about three in a group of 50 or 60 put their hands up. I explain that pressing the B key makes the screen go blank, which is one of the most useful tools for a presenter. As well as bringing attention back to yourself, it enables you to minimize distractions; you don't, for instance, want to leave a picture or diagram on screen if you were talking about it 10 minutes ago.

3. **Apply Best Presentation Practice.** All the principles we used to learn before PowerPoint was invented are still relevant. Arguably they are now more important than ever to ensure your performance is not swamped by the tools now available to you.

The construction process for Powerful PowerPoint involves a series of 10 progressive steps:

Step 1 – Take control

Steer well clear of your computer. PowerPoint will do all it can to "help" you by suggesting designs, offering templates and laying out colour palettes, but please don't be led by it. Think of yourself as a film director who would always make sure he has a story to tell before he gets out his cameras. Decide what you want and think visually, sketching it out in rough form, storyboard-style, before even thinking of opening up your computer.

Step 2 – Prime uses

Having decided to use PowerPoint, what are your prime uses going to be in this particular situation? Is it going to be as a visual aid, a takeaway document, a handout, or perhaps a combination of uses?

Remember that to work effectively as any of these formats, each really needs a different treatment. You don't, however, need to write multiple versions – Step 4 on Scripting shows you how to avoid that.

Step 3 – Structure

Start mapping out your structure – literally. Staying well away from your computer, draw out the key elements with pen and paper, visualizing it all as a route map. Think first of your objective as a destination you want your audience to reach and write it at the top of the page. Second, the starting point: consider how far your audience is from that destination currently and what are their current perceptions, buying habits and awareness in respect of the action you want them to take as defined in your objective. Write this at the bottom of the page.

You will find some sample scenarios below:

Scenario 1	Scenario 2	Scenario 3

1. Destinations (Objectives)

Sales for my new product, to establish 5% market share within two years	Support for my charity with donations short term and practical help longer term	Employment for a specific new job

2. Starting Points (The situation currently)

My product is almost unheard of outside a niche audience	My charity is a new one and has to compete with many deserving, long-established rivals	I have suitable experience but am rather mature compared with expectations and other applicants

The two important points at this stage are first, to ensure your destination includes a clear action point and, second, that you are realistic about your target audience's starting point. If, for instance, you know they don't like you, then be brutally honest with yourself and take that as the starting point. If you are not realistic you will be setting out on your journey from the wrong place, will be unlikely to engage your audience and will probably never reach your destination.

Next you need to map the ideas – roads and paths if you like, together with bridges to overcome specific obstacles – that will get you from your Starting Point to your Destination. Overlay these onto your map:

Scenario 1	Scenario 2	Scenario 3

1. Destinations

Sales for my new product, to establish 5% market share within two years	Support for my charity with donations short term and practical help longer term	Employment for a specific new job

3. Roads, Paths & Bridges (Ideas and tactics)

Point to lack of competitor innovation	Highlight charity's cause in a way that touches audience's hearts	Highlight experience
Highlight benefits enjoyed by niche audience & potential for broader audiences to enjoy those benefits	Make audience think twice about their traditional charity choices	Point to relevance of that experience
Make heroes of the niche audience – for wider audiences to aspire to	Seek ambassadors with high profiles and youth	Demonstrate young-at-heart attributes & third-party endorsement

2. Starting Points

My product is almost unheard of outside a niche audience	My charity is a new one and has to compete with many deserving, long-established rivals	I have suitable experience but am rather mature compared with expectations and other applicants

Finally, you need a compass that steers you from your Starting Point to your Destination. This is where your Single Simple Message (SSM) that I discussed in Chapter 3.1 comes in. If you don't already have an SSM look at your Roads/Paths/Bridges ideas and consider what phrase can act as an umbrella term to sum them all up in a memorable Single Simple Message. If you develop an SSM that covers most but not all of those ideas you might also like to consider whether those ideas are darlings that need to be killed off. Remember that the SSM is what keeps your audience – and you – on track; it really is like a compass.

Once you have developed an SSM overlay this onto your map, like this:

Scenario 1	**Scenario 2**	**Scenario 3**

1. Destinations

Sales for my new product to establish 5% market share within two years	Support for my charity with donations short term and practical help longer term	Employment for a specific new job

3. Roads, Paths & Bridges

Point to lack of competitor innovation	Highlight charity's cause in a way that touches audience's hearts	Highlight experience
Highlight benefits enjoyed by niche audience and the broader potential for those benefits	Make audience think twice about their traditional charity choices	Point to relevance of that experience
Make heroes of the niche audience – for wider audience to aspire to	Seek ambassadors with high profiles and youth	Demonstrate young-at-heart attributes & third-party endorsement

4. Single Simple Message (SSM)

Soon everyone's going to want one	A different way to make a difference	I was made for this job!

2. Starting Points

My product is almost unheard of outside a niche audience	My charity is a new one and has to compete with many deserving, long-established rivals	I have suitable experience but am rather mature compared with expectations and other applicants

The SSM for Scenario 1 aims to mark your product out almost as a well-kept secret, hence the reason most people have not heard of it to date. The audience has the chance to be in at the early stages, alongside these smart-minded early adopters. For Scenario 2 the SSM plays on the familiar phrase "making a difference" that is so important to encouraging charitable help. It encourages the audience to think twice before simply making their usual donation to the same old charity, while also fitting with the practical help – rather than simply money – that is sought in the longer term. Scenario 3 is about making yourself the obvious choice, even if they were expecting to hire someone rather different. Rather than looking for a job, you want *this* job.

Step 4 – Scripting

Now, finally, it is time to open up your computer. Let's assume you are creating:

- A visual aid that will support you as a presenter.
  and
- A document version that the audience can take away with them.

Bearing in mind the maxim that *a slide generally makes a lousy handout and a handout makes a lousy slide*, you need different treatments for each, but you do not need to do all the work twice. My recommendation is that you start scripting as follows:

---

1. Open up Notes area – BIG
2. Write in Notes area
3. Copy text to Slide area
4. Edit down to key words
5. Tidy up Notes area

This 1–5 listing is actually the precise wording of a PowerPoint slide I use when training. When I wrote it initially, however, it looked like this:

> - Open up the Notes area – nice and big – using arrow/lift device between Slide/Notes
> - Write in this area
>   (NB: It's easier to write/construct in the Notes area)
> - Once the words are broadly correct copy them to Slide area
> - Then, depending on the final uses you have planned:
>   – Edit down the words to a bare minimum for Presentation Aid
>   – Later you will also tidy up the Notes – according to how you will use them

Clearly that is far too many words to fit into a readable slide, but if you write your initial draft into the Notes area – which sits below the Slide area on the PowerPoint construction screen – you can simply let it all flow out without worrying about editing for the moment. If you then copy these words into the Slide area, you will find it quick and easy to edit them down into the bare essentials that support you as a presenter.

It also means you now have two different versions that can be printed out together on a Notes page and may well be suitable as the takeaway document. This way your audience receives an aide-memoire in the form of the slides they saw in your presentation, together with a fleshed-out version that can also be understood by anyone who did not attend your presentation. Two versions for the price – or effort – of one.

Word Density

What this technique also tackles head on is the fourth and the deadliest of the Seven Sins – that of Word Density. When using PowerPoint as a visual aid for speaker support it is essential that the words on screen are edited down to a bare minimum. The slides should be speaker support only; they should not be a prompt for you or a document. What do you want your audience to do? Look at and listen to you or sit there reading slides?

Slides full of bullet points can all too easily work against you because they create a barrier between presenter and audience. Invariably they make the atmosphere more stiff and formal and they make the audience work, creating frustration if they can't quite read them. So aim to make your words 24pt size or more and squint from the back of the room to check for readability.

We have all seen too many examples of what I am talking about here, but take a look at the one below that came straight from a leading London communications consultancy. It's certainly not the worst example I could show you, but it is typical of many presentations. This presentation had been used as a new business pitch and they asked for feedback as to how it might be improved. I have simply concealed the identity of the consultancy at the top and bottom of the slides.

Slide 1

DNA OF PERFECT PUB LANDLORD

- Work with occupational psychologist to unearth the skills and attributes of the most successful XX licensees
- From data, create pub landlord personality types to demonstrate broad range of opportunities
- Cross reference with consumer research to show what pub customers see as key traits of a good landlord
- Potential to use TV personalities as hooks to bring research to life
- Licensees act as spokespeople and case studies

My first comment came in the form of a question: Why have you used a grey font? "Because grey is our corporate colour, our managing director likes it," was their answer. "That's two good reasons to use grey," I said, "but please bear in mind that, while grey can look fine on a computer screen, it can become very wishy-washy when you print it out. And it can fade away almost completely when you put it through a projector onto a screen." So my advice for presentation purposes was to darken the font colour a little – probably to a dark grey rather than black.

The next and most important point was that the slides were all far too full of words to work effectively as presenter support. The presenter can say: "We will work with an occupational therapist to unearth …" All they need on the screen is a brief reminder of the point – as in slide 2.

Slide 2

DNA OF PERFECT PUB LANDLORD

- Work with occupational psychologist
- Create pub landlord personality types
- Cross reference with consumer research
- Potential to use TV personalities
- Licensees act as spokespeople and case studies

In fact, they don't need as much as that – they can make it even briefer as in slide 3.

Slide 3

> **DNA OF PERFECT PUB LANDLORD**
>
> • Occupational psychologist
> • Personality types
> • Consumer research
> • TV personalities
> • Licensees as spokespeople

They could write the bullet points in a font size that can be read by everyone so now the focus is primarily on the presenter. Notice also how much more powerful bullet points become when they appear on a single line.

Having edited, there is one more step to take. If you present your slides like this everyone is going to be reading ahead of what you are saying. You will be talking about occupational psychologists and many within the audience will be distracted by the thought of which TV personalities you are going to recommend. So use some simple animation to bring the points up one at a time, so creating a Single Point of Focus around what you are saying at this precise moment. You don't need to do this for every list of bullet points – sometimes you will be asking your audience to scan quickly over, say, a range of options, but it is good as a general rule. Do be sure to bring your points up one at a time when you want them to pay attention to each point individually.

Now you have a slide that builds up into brief reminders of each key point and the audience can see how they all hang together as you reach the final item.

With a little editing we have moved (see below) from slide 1 to slide 3 and now have a much more powerful tool with which to support a presenter. And this is before we have even considered how the whole thing could potentially be brightened up – with added clarification – with some visuals.

DNA OF PERFECT PUB LANDLORD

- Work with occupational psychologist to unearth the skills and attributes of the most successful XX licensees
- From data, create pub landlord personality types to demonstrate broad range of opportunities
- Cross reference with consumer research to show what pub customers see as key traits of a good landlord
- Potential to use TV personalities as hooks to bring research to life
- Licensees act as spokespeople and case studies

DNA OF PERFECT PUB LANDLORD

- Occupational psychologist
- Personality types
- Consumer research
- TV personalities
- Licensees as spokespeople

You can still use slide 1 for a document version, possibly presented under slide 3 as a twosome on a Notes page.

Finally on editing, if in doubt apply the "T-shirt test". How many words can you fit on a T shirt so that they are readable to a passerby?

Having got the scripting under way, there are a number of quite simple PowerPoint issues you need to consider:

Step 5 – Backgrounds

Keep them simple and distraction-free. By all means make them fit with your corporate imagery, but you really want your audience focusing on the content, so the background should be what magicians call "psychologically invisible" – in clear sight, but doing nothing to draw attention to itself.

Be wary of colours and tints. Again, deploy your corporate colours, but not at the expense of the readability of your content. I have frequently seen people use a photograph as a background. It may be something like a beautiful coastline to fit with their theme of, say, selling holiday homes abroad as an investment. The early bullet points stand out well because they are set against the sky. Subsequent bullet points are harder to read because the background has now become the darker blue of the sea. By the time we reach the concluding points at the bottom, the words have all but vanished into the rocks. You can of course alter the font colour but this would need to be multi-coloured in such an instance, which is a distraction in itself. The fact is that we usually read off white and there is a good reason for this.

Finally, corporate logos, which people often include in a corner, can become distracting, annoying and even intrusive, so plan these carefully if you intend to include them.

Step 6 – Bullet Points

Aim for a maximum of five bullet points,
- On two levels only
  - Like this
    » Not this – which is simply too much

Be wary of clichéd, inappropriate or ambiguous bullet-point styles. For instance, I tended to use dashes for sub-points until someone said: "I wish you wouldn't use those; I trained as an accountant and every time I see one I think 'minus'." You can actually make bullet points out of almost anything you want – your logo, for instance – but I would advise against getting too clever or fancy. By their very nature bullet points need to be small, so anything other than the simplest shape will soon look very indistinct. Like backgrounds, bullet points should really be psychologically invisible – in clear view, but not demanding any specific attention.

We have already seen that:
- bullet points can have much greater impact when written on one line

So eliminate all but the most vital words:
- one-line bullets for greatest impact

To help you in the elimination process don't worry about grammar, forget about the definite and indefinite article – *the, a, an* – and use symbols and abbreviations such as "&" for "and" wherever possible.

Step 7 – Animation

The simple rule here is: if in doubt, avoid it. I have discussed the importance of creating a Single Points of Focus around the bullet point you are currently discussing and that generally requires a simple animation option such as "Appear".

Here again there is a great danger of being guided and even cajoled by PowerPoint, which offers you every possible kind of animation effect, because it *can*. I said that Austin and Gaskins put rather too much emphasis on technology and not enough on Best Presentation Practice when they invented PowerPoint; well, their successors really went to town when it came to the animation palette. Some of the effects can actually be quite useful – if applied in small doses. If, for instance, you have a really special press cutting to show it might be appropriate to have it spinning into view like an old movie effect. What you don't want to do is then apply the same effect to the second, third and fourth cuttings on display.

The reason it works the first time is largely due to a mix of surprise and difference; if you repeat the effect it is neither surprising nor different. Indeed, once people know what effect is coming, you will soon find that it slows down the pace of the presentation as everyone waits for the animation effect to do its little act. Animation can quickly become annoying and distracting. I have said, "You are the show, PowerPoint has a supporting role at best." Rather like a traditional magician's assistant we want PowerPoint to make us look good, but not to start trying for laughs and applause itself.

On a more serious note, you can often find that animation simply doesn't match with the rhythm of your speech. So your careful synchronization with the screen image is wasted and the effect on you as a speaker is actually rather unnerving. I demonstrate this point with my Winston Churchill "Fight them on the beaches" spoof. I start by speaking with Churchill's timing, but deliberately falter as I have to wait for the next bullet point to come bouncing into position.

Step 8 – Graphs and Charts

Keep graphs and charts as simple as possible for presentation purposes because you lose impact once you go beyond four or five elements. Again, a more detailed version, together with all the correct references, can be issued in the takeaway document.

The question of readability needs particular attention with PowerPoint because what works on a page or even a computer will not necessarily work effectively when projected onto a screen, where fine detail and essential information on the axes may be hard to read. Think back here to Chapter 4.6 and the lesson I learned at The Magic Circle from Ali Bongo: "Thickness of line is more important than sheer scale." I realized how particularly valuable that tip was the moment I next used PowerPoint. If you ask PowerPoint for a line graph, for instance, it offers you a basic version which you need to remodel to your own needs.

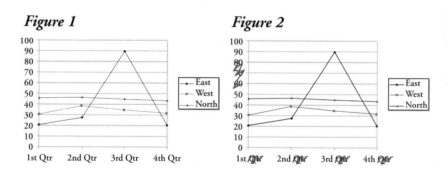

Figure 1 *Figure 2*

This (Figure 1) may look fine on the computer screen and when printed on a page, but try projecting it; because the lines are very thin you can barely see them. So, as well as keeping graphs and charts simple, give serious consideration to thickening the lines and emboldening any data (see Figure 2). If the audience can't read the detail, your point is unlikely to come across.

Finally, clear any clutter. How many of the numbers from 1–100 along one axis do you actually need to show? In this case nothing actually scores between 50 and 90 so why do you need all the numbers? Also, the horizontal axis shows 1ˢᵗ Qtr, 2ⁿᵈ Qtr, 3ʳᵈ Qtr, 4ᵗʰ Qtr. Why keep repeating Qtr using up valuable space and creating distractions?

Step 9 – Visuals for PowerPoint

Visuals are all about creating and adding impact, the topic that I cover in Chapter 4.6 with tips on how visuals can help in terms of: *clarification, conveying a lot of detail, reinforcing similes and metaphors* and *detail that begs visual questions* .

Additionally, there are specific ways in which visuals can be deployed within PowerPoint:

- As a device for **subtle repetition** – I have already discussed the need for repetition and how it must be stealthy to be effective rather than potentially annoying. A visual image that keeps reappearing, possibly in diminished form, can achieve this.
- To underpin a **running theme** – visuals can depict the theme and evolve through the presentation to bring the theme alive. I could, for instance, use a visual device in the *Construction* section of my training whereby I start with a pile of bricks and this gradually transforms into a house as I progress.
- As a **pacing device** – visuals can be used to depict the start and continuation of "chapters" or subject headings. My training sessions, for instance, are divided into *Construction, Preparation* and *Delivery,* and the accompanying PowerPoint presentation has an appropriate visual that flags up each section and then runs in diminished form in a corner until the topic changes.

- To **break up and brighten up** – what can otherwise be an endless bunch of bullet points. Once all the above have been taken into account you should look through the presentation to see where it could be brightened up further and where opportunities for visuals present themselves naturally. Also, check for consistency and insert a visual where any significant non-illustrated gaps occur.

Step 10 – Consistency

Finally – and it should be a final step – you need to check for consistency throughout your presentation, specifically in these areas:

- Wording in terms of style and grammatical construction
- Bullet point style
- Weight and size of text and headings
- Colours
- Spacing and general layout

The simple answer to achieving most of this is actually to work to a well-designed template, which does most of the work for you and instills a sense of discipline. Checking for consistency also gives you one final opportunity to sharpen your words and word count, taking out anything superfluous, so creating maximum impact.

In a nutshell

PowerPoint can be a wonderful tool if you follow simple procedures to keep it in its rightful place and make it *work* for you, not drive you.

PART II

PREPARATION

I prefaced Part I with a statement of my belief that the three elements of *Construction, Preparation* and *Delivery* carry equal importance. By now the importance of real time invested in *Construction* should be self-apparent, but you may be thinking: Do I really need to devote much time to *Preparation?* I have a good PA and I've got a business to run, surely I can leave the *Preparation* to others?

Having a good team to help you is a definite bonus, but just as a pilot makes his own pre-flight checks and a high-wire walker is the one to tighten the rope, a magician will always set up his own props. If these sound rather extreme as parallel situations, just think about how certain presentations really have been a matter of life or death business-wise to people you know or have read about, even if it has yet to happen to you. Then think about how easily it could have gone the other way if some tiny detail had been overlooked. Maybe you were so busy rehearsing that you forgot to book the car. Your key target turned out to be Scandinavian so his name was spelt "Andersen" not "Anderson" as you assumed and printed on the screen and in your document. You have mis-timed your presentation so that, while you appear to have recovered from mis-spelling Mr Andersen's name, he has to leave before you reach your big conclusion.

We are regularly told that in business it is the little things that can make all the difference to achieving success, and this also holds true for disaster, where a tiny detail, such as a single letter in a person's name, can sway everything in the wrong direction. Magicians are keenly aware of the principles of Murphy's Law – *Anything that can go wrong will go wrong* – because the nature of their job brings so much potential for calamity of all kinds. In fact, one of the earliest references to Murphy's Law in academic studies is to a 1908 editorial that British stage magician Nevil Maskelyne wrote in the Magic Circle's magazine *The Magic Circular*. He said:

> It is an experience common to all men to find that, on any special occasion, such as the production of a magical effect for the first time in public, everything that *can* go wrong *will* go wrong. Whether we must attribute this to the malignity of matter or to the total depravity of inanimate things, whether the exciting cause is hurry, worry, or what not, the fact remains.

The important point here, apart from the need to anticipate problems in advance, is that problems are all the more likely to occur when you are tense and nervous. So problems are most likely to occur on occasions that are vitally important to you.

Chapter 7
PRE-PRODUCTION

Who, where and how long?;
equipment; addressing nerves

Before embarking on any kind of business communication there are three essential questions to ask yourself: *Who? Where?* and *How long?* Close attention paid to each of these will help you tailor your presentation more precisely to the specific situation; conversely, any lack of attention in these areas could easily be your undoing.

7.1 Who and how many are you seeing?

If you are only beginning to address the "Who" element at this stage you have your priorities in the wrong order. As the most important factor in any communication, the audience should be driving the *Construction* process. By now, therefore, you should have addressed key factors including:

- Expectations and perceptions you are triggering – (Rule 1 – *What "files" am I opening in the minds of my audience?*) – *Chapter 2.1*
- Elements of Prestige, Atmosphere & Environment and Desire that can help to either build up or play down those expectations and perceptions (Rule 2) – *Chapter 2.1*
- Building on what your audience already knows (Rule 3 – Familiar reference points) – *Chapter 2.2*
- Elements that need adjusting – jargon? complexity? cultural references? and so on – to more closely suit this particular audience – *Chapter 2.3*

- Making your message important to this audience – probably through personalization (Rule 4) – *Chapter 2.4*
- The approach they will respond to best – dramatic or straight? detailed or concise? new technology or traditional? – *Chapter 2.5*

Now is the time to check that you have fully considered every way in which your presentation can be tailored specifically to the needs of the audience you are about to address.

7.2 **Where are you seeing them?**

Again, before you start constructing your presentation you should have at least a general idea of where you will be presenting. Think back to the story of the pitch to Sir Richard Branson in the relaxed atmosphere of his home; this illustrates how important the venue can be to the general nature of your presentation – it may even dictate it.

I always urge people to visit the venue in advance of their presentation if at all possible. This enables you to assess some fundamentals such as: identifying the position and benefits of key focal points; assigning presenter and audience positions; deciding on the scale of visual aids; and liaising with any technical crew.

Venue knowledge is key to addressing nerves

The benefits of visiting a venue, however, run much deeper than this. Seeing the venue can also be of great help in addressing any nerves that you have about giving the presentation. It's perfectly natural to be nervous before a presentation, and experience does not always help – Tony Blair says he still gets nervous before giving a speech. For the record, the amygdala, which sits at the base of our brains, is the guilty party. It is this that sends us into fight-or-flight mode when we sense danger. It creates a hormone rush all around our bodies, giving us extra strength to either fight the threat or run away from it. Meanwhile, other essential functions – such as the ability to speak properly – shut down. All of which is very interesting, but you are about to give a presentation that is crucial to your career and your nerves are playing havoc – what can you actually *do*?

What you need to understand is that the greatest cause of nerves when it comes to stage fright is fear of the unfamiliar. So you need to make the situation familiar to yourself – by seeing the venue. Aside from the basic planning benefits detailed above, this enables you to visualize the situation as you prepare and rehearse. Rather than having indistinct possibilities of what it might be like churning away in your brain, you can visualize exactly what it actually is going to be like and replicate that in every detail as you rehearse. Gradually you become more and more comfortable with the situation because it is increasingly familiar to you.

I have proved the benefits of seeing the venue so as to make it familiar on a number of occasions. One of the most striking was when I took my exam to achieve full membership of The Magic Circle. I was going to have to perform for around 12 minutes in the Devant Room at the Magic Circle HQ in London, in front of an array of members and surrounded by icons of magical history. This was a terrifying thought – I would be performing at the HQ of the world's foremost magic society in front of people who would know every technique I was using and much more besides. Fortunately, I had a mentor in Jack Delvin, one of the great stalwarts of The Magic Circle, who became President in 2009. He had already coached me at home and he recommended that the final stage of preparation should be to actually do a run through in the Devant Room. So I set up in the right spot, already appreciating how useful it was to get a feel for the surroundings, the lighting and the acoustics. What I wasn't expecting on this occasion was for Jack to shout out to everyone on the premises, "OK everybody, come and watch a magic show." I was suddenly faced with magicians of all sizes and shapes, some of them the best in their field and one or two really quite famous. I had no choice but to get on and do it, but I survived the ordeal. When I came to do the actual exam a fortnight later – in the same place and in front of similar people – the fear factor was largely removed because I had been through it all before. And I passed the exam.

Of course, it's not always possible to check out the venue in advance, but more often than not you can. If, for instance, you are due to pitch for business you can always ask at the briefing meeting: "If we are invited to pitch, will it be in this room?" or "Before we leave, would you mind showing us the room you will use for the pitch?" When conference venues or hotels are used you can often look up specific rooms on the internet and get a reasonable feel for them.

I felt uneasy when preparing to present at the Communication Directors Forum on board a ship. Seeing this venue in advance simply wasn't possible because it was somewhere in the South Atlantic. There was one particular incident, however, where I felt unusually nervous. I was asked to speak on my usual topic of applying the Rules of Magic to business communication, but this invitation came from Adrian Chiles for his BBC TV programme *Working Lunch*. I had never done TV before, so for the first time in ages the nerves set in and I panicked. Follow your own advice, I thought, and see the venue. But you can't really go poking around the BBC. Then I realized that of course I could see the venue. By recording the show I could easily work out that I would either be put at the big table from which they open and close the show or, more likely, I would be put at the smaller coffee table that they use in the middle of the show. Then I could consider: Would I be able to set myself up left-to-right? Could I reach across if I need to interact with, say, a magic trick? Would the camera pick up any props I use? Most of all, though, I realized I was going to have to do all of this sitting down, which is an un-natural position for me. It would feel strange and un-nerving to be doing my regular spiel from a seated position when I usually work standing up. So I set myself up at home exactly as I expected to be in the *Working Lunch* studio and rehearsed like that for a week beforehand. When I came to do it for real it was easy – because the scenario was so familiar to me.

7.3 **How long have you got?**

At the *Construction* stage you will already have addressed the key factor:

> Editing. You need to kill your darlings – stories, facts and visual aids that are dear to your heart but have to be cut if they do not add directly to what you are seeking to communicate. Magicians are probably more aware than anybody that "If it doesn't add, it will detract."

At this stage you will probably need to kill some more darlings because in most situations timing is critical. You will have been allocated a set amount of time, and exceeding that time will almost certainly annoy your audience – it may also throw the rest of everyone's itinerary into confusion. And remember: firsts and lasts stay with the audience so you have planned to build to a climax that sends them away with your key messages. If you are forced to rush or even cut your Outro, you will be robbed of your climax. Remember also that most people will thank you for coming in a little under time, which also introduces a degree of flexibility.

So, insist on being given a time allocation, then time your rehearsals carefully and be prepared to kill some more darlings.

7.4 **Equipment**

MANY MAGICIANS PRIDE THEMSELVES ON WORKING WITH AS FEW PROPS AS POSSIBLE AND MAGIC DEALERS PROMOTE THEIR

WARES WITH LINES SUCH AS "PACKS FLAT, PLAYS BIG". THERE
ARE NUMEROUS ADVANTAGES TO THIS APPROACH, BUT THE
BIGGEST IS THAT THERE IS LESS TO GO WRONG AND LESS TO
DEPEND UPON IF IT ALL GOES MISSING.

The most important tip about equipment is to avoid being ambushed. Be very wary of technology, which is probably the greatest of all proving grounds for Murphy's Law – *If it can go wrong, it will go wrong.* How many presentations have you seen where technology let the speaker down? Even if the problem can be corrected, the speaker is usually left flustered and playing catch up.

So keep it simple. If, for instance, I want to show a video clip, I tend to run it from a separate DVD player rather than off my laptop. That seems clunky to some, but I feel much more confident knowing that I can make an absolutely smooth transition from PowerPoint to DVD and back. What's more, I can actually see that the DVD clip is set in the right place and ready to run. Similarly, for sound I tend to use an iPod and sound dock rather than depend on my laptop to perform an additional function.

Whenever using any equipment ask yourself: To what extent is this really adding to the impact of my presentation? Is it worth the additional work and stress that it creates? Might it even detract from the main thrust of my presentation?

Finally, pack a parachute. What will you do if something goes wrong? Clearly, if you have a presentation on a laptop, then you should always have a copy on a memory stick. If your laptop fails or is lost you can plug the memory stick into a borrowed (or spare) laptop. But what if there is a complete power failure or loss of key visual aids? Could you give a credible and effective presentation without them? If you have considered this, there is probably a way that you can. If you have not considered such a scenario and it occurs, you will almost certainly be left floundering.

To make your life as stress-free as possible I recommend carrying your own equipment. I do this whenever possible – I take everything including projector and screen. That way, I know exactly how to operate the equipment, I can be assured that everything is compatible and I can have the screen at the best vantage point rather than in a fixed position determined by some office manager in the dim and distant past.

Screens and positioning

When planning for projection screens there is a simple formula called the "Six Rule" – the distance from the screen to the furthest person in the room should be less than the screen width multiplied by six. So a 10-metre room needs a screen of 1.5 metres or more. Also, corner positioning can often provide the greatest visibility and space for the presenter to manoeuvre.

Flat screen TVs are, of course, becoming increasingly prevalent, but given the choice I still prefer to work with a projector where possible. Although they get bigger by the day, flat screen TVs still tend to be considerably smaller than a projected image and have little scope to vary the size of the picture. Furthermore, they are often fixed to a wall that may be some way from your audience; even if they are mounted on a stand they tend to be difficult to move. Roll-down screens may also be in a fixed position, but you still have the option to bring your own screen and place it in your preferred position. I often move a screen much closer to the audience than where it has been set up.

It is definitely a good idea to work from your own laptop and to carry certain essentials such a mains extension lead, projector extension lead, simple toolkit and gaffer tape. Also, my favourite piece of kit – a gender changer. This is a simple device that enables you to join a projector lead (running to your laptop) to an extension. This means that you can position yourself where you want to be (ideally left-to-right with the screen from the audience's view) rather than tethered by the (often short) lead provided by the venue. Remember also that if you are using a Mac you will need an adapter to cope with the Mac's digital sockets.

All of which begs one final question: Now that you are able to position yourself where you really want to be, what are you going to put your laptop on so that you can see and reach it from your preferred speaking position? You may be provided with a lectern. It may be that the main table is suitably positioned. It may even be that they have a small, tall, foldaway table available. That is leaving it to chance, though, and it's much better if you carry your own solution. Being a magician I am fortunate enough to have a Harbin table, a small table that folds away into almost nothing. These are expensive, difficult to find and quite fragile, so keep an eye out in furniture shops for something small and foldable.

7.5 Specific causes of nerves

As a final point on pre-production, there are a number of specific factors – in addition to the fear of the unfamiliar – that make us nervous. These include:

- Not knowing your material
- Presenting to people you know – a blank canvas is much easier because you are not constantly considering the perceptions and personal agendas of the people in front of you
- Giving someone else's presentation – because how ever well you know the subject matter it will not fit your own rhythms and nuances
- Unexpected interruptions
- Equipment difficulties

The good news is that rehearsal and planning can reduce or even eliminate all of these, so pointing to additional reasons to address the issue of nerves at this stage.

In a nutshell

Small details that might not even occur to you can make or break your presentation. Identifying them keeps you in control and brings the additional benefit of calming your nerves.

Chapter 8
REHEARSAL

Replicating the scenario; rehearsal routine, rehearsal specifics; prompt aids; planning for problems; the "Starbucks Test"

8.1 Replicating the scenario

THERE IS A STANDARD JOKE WITHIN THE MAGIC FRATERNITY THAT YOU CAN TELL THE SIZE OF AN INEXPERIENCED MAGICIAN'S LIVING ROOM BY NOTING THE AMOUNT OF SPACE HE WORKS WITHIN ON STAGE. THE POINT IS THAT HE HAS REHEARSED, BUT NOT REPLICATED THE SITUATION WITHIN WHICH HE WILL BE WORKING.

I have discussed the great value of making the situation familiar – to overcome nerves as well as maximize effectiveness. So you should replicate everything as closely as possible, and I mean everything: *layout, technical equipment, visual aids and props, time of day, clothes.*

If it sounds like this is taking things unnecessarily far, let me tell you two stories. The first concerns a top London PR consultancy that was staging a trade press launch for a world-famous confectionary company in the Pavilion at London Zoo. The venue was chosen, no doubt, for its originality and the attractive, light, airy room. Now, I was once asked to nominate my favourite features for the ideal training room and I put "room with windows" at the top of my list; nothing saps energy more than sitting in a windowless room for long periods. At the same time, the words "light and airy" also trigger a danger signal to me.

On this occasion the brand manager opened his PowerPoint and all was going well. PowerPoint was essential to his presentation because he had a lot of graphs to show, figures to compare and packaging innovations for quite small products to display. After a few minutes he made a big point about the state of the market, concluding with the words "as you can see here" to introduce a graph. At that precise moment, bright sunshine came out from behind a big cloud and his graph was wiped out almost completely by bright rays shining across the screen. So precise was the timing of the sun's arrival that, to the presenter's credit, he hardly missed a beat as he said "as you can see here ... or perhaps not." The rest of his presentation, however, was literally wiped out – by sunlight. Becoming increasingly flustered with expressions such as, "You can't see it here, but ..." he was not helped at all by the increasingly frantic and fruitless attempts by his PR team to block out the sun. The fact was that they were unlucky – it was a dark, November day until that unexpected burst of sunlight. And they *had* rehearsed, but at a different time of day, when the sun sits in another part of the sky.

The clothing lesson is one I learned from my own bitter experience. It is standard practice to advise against wearing a new outfit when you have to make a presentation because you are seeking to make the scenario as familiar as possible and wearing a new outfit is going to work against that. My particular clothing problem really came down to props and equipment management. I was working in a large lecture theatre where I knew they would ask me to use a lapel microphone, for which a battery pack needs to go inside a discreet pocket. I was working without a jacket so I planned to put the battery pack in my left rear trouser pocket, leaving the right rear trouser pocket clear to store some intricately arranged cards that I needed to produce smoothly as part of a surprise climax.

When it came to the day, however, I was wearing the "wrong" trousers – they only had one rear pocket and I needed that for my cards; nothing else could go in that pocket for fear of the cards catching on it as I produced them. So I tucked the battery pack into my waistband and mid-way through my presentation it started sliding down my trouser leg. I carried on regardless and I don't think anyone noticed, but I was slightly unnerved and certainly constrained in my movement thereafter.

Replicating the scenario – as precisely as possible – identifies the gremlins and, above all, helps to make the situation familiar.

8.2 Rehearsal routine

"CLARITY TRAPS", WHERE A LACK OF ENUNCIATION ON SPECIFIC WORDS MEANS THEY ARE MIS-HEARD BY THE AUDIENCE, ARE COMMON WHEN THE SPEAKER IS UNDER PRESSURE, BUT MAGICIANS USE THIS TO THEIR ADVANTAGE. IF A VOLUNTEER IS ASKED TO NAME THEIR FAVOURITE PLAYING CARD AND CHOOSES, SAY, THE ACE OF HEARTS, THE MAGICIAN MIGHT PROUDLY PRODUCE A SINGLE CARD FROM AN ENVELOPE, REVEALING IT BE THE *EIGHT* OF HEARTS. FEIGNING HAVING MIS-HEARD HE WILL THEN DO SOMETHING TRULY MAGICAL AND TRANSFORM THE CARD INTO THE CORRECT ACE OF HEARTS CHOICE.

In an ideal world – and I fully accept that we rarely live in such a world – you should go through three stages of preparation and then come to a definite halt.

Stage One – Start rehearsing on your own, introducing your aids and replicating the scenario as early as possible. You can achieve a great deal at this stage because you can rehearse in an un-self-conscious manner, experimenting and making mistakes along the way without embarrassment.

Stage Two – Invite some sympathetic ears, someone who will listen from an objective viewpoint, suggesting where clarification is needed and commenting on the effectiveness of different aids.

Stage Three – By now you should have a well-refined presentation that is nearly ready to go live, so put it through its paces to find out how robust it is. Ask someone – ideally two or three people well versed in the subject matter – to ask some really difficult questions, find faults and even heckle in some appropriate places. Here again, familiarization is the key; if you have already had the heaviest grilling possible, you will be going over familiar territory when it comes to the real thing. Furthermore, you will have some pre-prepared defence mechanisms to deflect any flak that comes your way.

Then you need to stop, ideally adopting what magicians call the Hollingworth Rule, which says "Stop rehearsing 24 hours in advance." People in marketing agencies laugh when I introduce them to the Hollingworth Rule, exclaiming: "You're joking; we're still writing the document 24 hours in advance." Having worked in that world myself I know what they mean, but it's a good principle to at least aspire to. Guy Hollingworth is a highly respected member of The Magic Circle who could make a good living on several continents working as a magician; instead, his time is devoted mainly to practising as a barrister. He says that, just as it is generally counter-productive to cram for exams right up until the last moment, rehearsing in the final 24 hours is unlikely to be helpful. Instead you can use the time to visualize the presentation going well and in doing so keep the adrenaline rush under control so that you can use it to positive effect.

Finally, remember to keep timing yourself. The problem is that our brains play tricks with us when it comes to presentations and timing. You can almost guarantee that your own presentation will seem either longer or shorter than it really is. Once you have it right, build in a little leeway to allow for the discussion and small diversions that will emerge naturally in a presentation that is flowing well.

Rehearsal specifics

Intro and Outro – Focus on these more than anything else. Remember Rule 13: *Firsts and lasts are remembered.* If you get off to a good start you should sail through; with a bad start you will be playing catch-up throughout. And your Outro is your big, and final, opportunity for your audience to understand your key message, remember it and act upon it.

Get used to speaking the words – Don't just read them; speak them out loud to avoid surprises. Some words may unexpectedly turn into tongue twisters when you say them out loud and others might appear in awkward juxtaposition.

Speak a little slower than normal conversation – Rather than 170–180 words per minute speak at 120–130 words per minute. Bear in mind that when you are nervous and excited the heart speeds up and with it your speech rate. You may need to work on slowing down your speech; one way is to build in deliberate pauses, which are useful and effective in their own right. We shall look in more detail at pauses in Part III when we come to *Delivery*.

Emphasis in the right place – The emphasis on or within specific words is easily misplaced when you are under pressure. There is a significant difference between, say, "*This* is really important" and "This is *really important*," so rehearse any potential danger areas carefully and maybe even re-write them if necessary.

Similarly, while negatives should generally be avoided, when you do need to use them make sure the prefix is fully enunciated. For example, un-necessary can easily sound like necessary (the opposite) unless the "un" is emphasized.

Clarity traps can also be found in numbers, letters and expectations. For instance, 50 can easily be mis-heard as 15; *F* often sounds like *S*;

and because, until recently anyway, we were more used to hearing about millions than billions, the latter may be interpreted as the former.

Get a feel for the equipment – Be sure you know how to operate any equipment you are using. You should be able to do this without thinking, because on the day your mind will be on much more important matters. In particular you should be able to manipulate your slide changer in such a way that your audience doesn't even notice you are using one. Any fumbling will create a distraction for your audience and be un-nerving for you.

Plan the handling of your visual aids – Chapter 13.3 looks at how to ensure you display your aids properly. But you also need to think at this stage about the practicalities of where you are going to keep your aids prior to revealing them, whether they need special support while displaying them and where you are going to put them when you move onto the next point. The best magicians know that this sort of attention to detail can make all the difference between smooth delivery and distracting clumsiness. The point is that picking up, displaying and putting away should all be "psychologically invisible" – you shouldn't notice the movements, with the result that full focus remains on your communication.

Plan for questions in four ways

1. **Obvious questions** – How ever comprehensive you make your presentation, there will always be a variety of fairly obvious questions that you can anticipate, so craft and rehearse answers.
2. **Difficult questions** – Work with colleagues to brainstorm the difficult questions you could be asked, then craft and rehearse answers.

In both these cases you should work with fairly broad categories of question. Typically you will find that most questions will probably fall into about half a dozen different categories. If you have a well-rehearsed answer for each category you should be able to cope well with variations within that category, using essentially the same answer.

3. **Frequently Asked Questions** – Essentially these are soft versions of the obvious questions and can be used in presentation situations if you find that no one asks a question. It often happens (and for a variety of reasons) and always creates an uncomfortable feeling for all concerned. To avoid a question gap or silence, have some Frequently Answered Questions up your sleeve and break the silence as soon as it becomes evident that no questions are forthcoming with an opener like: "Something I am often asked is …" You then pose your own question so it is easy to answer, which means you are maintaining control in more ways than one. Also, by that time someone has probably plucked up the courage to ask a real question and a flow of enquiries usually follows; it's the fear of being the first that tends to block the start of questions.

4. **News-related questions** – Remember to have at least a quick scan of the news headlines on the day of your presentation. You will feel too busy to do this, but those headlines are going to be at the front of the minds of your audience so you may get questions relating to them. I have even had clients whose own company has featured in the news on the morning of their presentation and not all of the team have been aware of the fact until the Q&As started.

Finally, decide whether you are happy to take questions as you progress through the presentation or prefer your audience to wait until later. There is no right or wrong to this, unless you have a particularly tight time schedule, in which case you need to keep to a strict format of questions in a pre-defined slot. I quite like taking questions as I go as it gives me feedback and brings a less formal feel to the proceedings. Some questioners, however, can be a nuisance and show little respect for the presenter or fellow audience members, so you need to retain control. If it becomes obvious that they are continually jumping the gun on things you are about to discuss it is best to tell such people that all of their enquiries so far are covered within the presentation, so please hold back for a moment on the questions.

8.3 Prompt Aids

BEING SEEN TO WORK FROM NOTES IS NOT REALLY APPROPRIATE FOR MAGICIANS AS IT DOESN'T QUITE FIT WITH THE NOTION OF MAKING PREDICTIONS, LET ALONE MEMORY FEATS OR MIND READING. MAGICIANS DO, HOWEVER, USE ALL KIND OF PROMPTS AND MNEMONIC DEVICES. FOR EXAMPLE, CARDS SET UP IN CHaSeD ORDER = CLUBS, HEARTS, SPADES, DIAMONDS.

The first thing to make clear here is that it is perfectly acceptable to use notes. While people may marvel at those who deliver a perfect presentation without notes, there is absolutely no shame in using them. A few highly experienced speakers have even adopted the tactic of using fake notes – a few cards that they shuffle around – in order to overcome the perception that they have not bothered to prepare a special speech for the occasion. As long as you don't read directly from them, it is all right to look down at your notes periodically; indeed this can act as an aid to punctuation and even eye contact.

The key to an effective prompt is to keep it small and stiff – ideally A5 size (210 X 148mm). The stiffness of the card makes it easy to get the prompt in and out of your pocket, stops it flopping out of view and avoids rustling near microphones.

The best format is a simple map in a large typeface with generous spacing so that a simple glance down at the card gets you back on track if you suddenly have a blank as to what comes next. I call this a "Confidence Card" because knowing that there is a safety net in your hand should you need it makes you more self-assured, with the result that you probably don't need it. The map format is the opposite of the sort of notes devices that most people arrive with when I first train them. Often they have a complete page – or pages – of closely set type. Assuming they don't go so far as to read directly from their notes, what tends to happen is that they freeze for a moment as nerves get the better of them and their mind goes blank as to what comes next. Looking down at their notes for guidance is no help whatsoever because all they see is a page full of small print, when what they need is simply a key word – literally a prompt – to trigger a memory of what comes next.

On the following two pages, you will see the front and back of a Confidence Card I made for myself. On this occasion the challenge was not one of being unsure of what to say; it was much more a question of having too much to say for the time allotted and I had to be very strict about editing myself. I had been invited to appear on the Chris Evans Show on BBC Radio 2 and they told me I had three and a half minutes to talk about how the Rules of Magic could help business people to communicate during a recession. This was a very tall order – the shortest talk I do is 45 minutes long. The opportunity of speaking directly to some six million people was, however, too good to miss, so I treated the whole thing as a combined Intro and Outro, with precise scripting and a map-style prompt to keep me on track.

"In a recession," I said, "business people need to **de-clutter** their communication and they can **learn from the best magicians** in achieving that. The trouble is that in recession people panic and start portraying themselves as **jacks of all trades**, with the result that they become indistinct and nobody notices them. Magicians work hard to create a **Single Point of Focus** and business people should do the

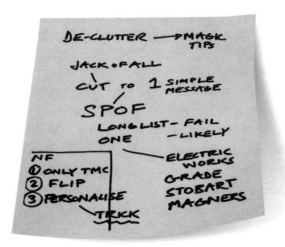

same – focusing on **a single simple message** that locks them into the consciousness of their target audience."

At the bottom I had two small lists in case 1) Evans asked me how I **differentiate myself**, and 2) he asked for **examples** of applying this principle successfully within the business world. That way there would be no need to rack my brain for a suitable answer as my eye could go straight to a list of options.

Similarly, on the reverse side I had a list of examples of the Rules of Magic, should I be questioned about those: *Firsts & lasts; Left-to right; Words That Paint Pictures* and so on. I had no time to think or run through a list of potential answers in my mind. I had to go straight to a solution and these were the examples that I believed could be communicated most quickly and effectively over the radio.

My Confidence Card did the trick for me; I found I could communicate my quite complex subject matter in a short timeframe, provided that I planned for it and had had an appropriate support mechanism. Proof that it worked came with the long list of emails that awaited me when I returned from the radio studio. Among them were offers of work across Europe, invitations to speak and enquiries

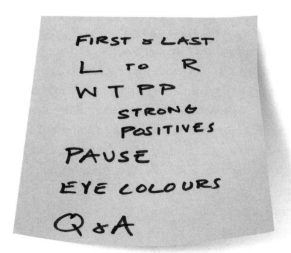

as to whether I had written a book. You are now reading the response to those latter enquiries.

When not to look at your notes

You should specifically avoid looking at notes when either:

> you need to indicate that something comes straight from the heart – looking at notes would clearly undermine you.

or:

> you are referring to crucial facts (or names) about your own company or your client's company – you cannot expect to create empathy if you appear unable to commit these to memory.

When to make a point of letting your notes show

Conversely, a very effective presentation tactic can be to make a point of referring to notes – even displaying the note clearly – so as to underline its authenticity. The most common use of this technique is when quoting directly from a source. If the quote is relatively long it may not be credible that you can remember it precisely, especially if it is not going to display well on a screen. Picking up the original source – perhaps a book – and quoting directly from it is both a useful prompt and a convincing visual aid. I use the technique when I refer to my son's school report when talking about negatives. I have actually committed the words to memory but I believe the small dramatic gesture of reading from the report itself adds a little authenticity to the story. Similarly, when Alastair Campbell gives his talk about "10 lessons" he learned from his time as Tony Blair's head of communications, he holds up a small a piece of paper on which he said he wrote the list of 10 lessons as he learned them. He even says he came across the list when he returned to Downing Street in 2010 and cleared his old office while helping with the General Election.

Prompt Aids for PowerPoint

When using PowerPoint you have the additional requirement of co-ordinating your words with the slides. You *must* be aware of what is coming next because the more you can synchronize what you say precisely with what you show, the more impact you will create.

Happily, technology now comes to the speaker's aid in this respect. If you use a Mac then the necessary technology is already built-in for PowerPoint and Keynote in the form of *Presenter Tools*. Switching to *Slide Show* simply shows the presenter on their monitor what everyone else is seeing on the big screen. Clicking *View*, followed by *Presenter Tools*, however, brings up a different format on the monitor – one that is designed specifically to help the presenter.

The top left-hand corner of *Presenter Tools* displays a clock that can be set either as a timer or to show the current time. Down the left-hand side the presenter can see the run of slides. The rest of the screen is divided into a big view of the slide currently being projected, underneath which is displayed the Notes section relating to that slide. You can even overlay another small version of the next slide coming up.

Presenter Tools is undoubtedly one of the most useful aids available to a presenter. I used to struggle with paper notes on top of my keyboard that needed adjusting every time I tailored a presentation. Then I discovered Apple's Mac computers with the facility built-in and as a result I have been using Macs ever since. At the time of writing similar aids are available on some PCs under the tab *Presenter View* and they can be found on Open Office Impress under *Presenter Screen*.

In summary, the *Presenter Tools* function enables a presenter to simply glance at their screen and:

- Know the current time or how much time has elapsed.
- See the current slide showing on the big screen.
- See the notes relating to that slide.
- See the previous slide and the slide coming up.

I recommend *Presenter Tools* to anyone using PowerPoint or Keynote for their presentations.

8.4 **Planning for problems**

THINGS CERTAINLY GO WRONG FOR MAGICIANS – QUITE FREQUENTLY IN FACT. FURTHERMORE, GREMLINS SHOW LITTLE RESPECT FOR SKILL OR EXPERIENCE – THE REALITY IS THAT TOP MAGICIANS ARE AFFLICTED ALMOST AS MUCH AS HUMBLER PRACTITIONERS, BUT THEY RARELY LET IT SHOW. THEY ANTICIPATE PROBLEMS AND HAVE A RANGE OF "OUTS" – WAYS TO GET THEMSELVES OUT OF THE PROBLEM SO THAT YOU WOULD NEVER REALIZE ANYTHING WAS AMISS.

I say "planning for problems" rather than anything more positive, such as planning to *avert* problems, because, as we know from Murphy's Law, the one thing you can be sure of is that things *will* go wrong. This applies how ever diligent you have been in your planning – you can minimize the potential for problems but you can never eliminate them completely.

Of course, the more risks you take, the more you increase the likelihood of things going awry. When I say risks I mean the introduction of anything beyond the simplest scenario of you standing up and speaking. I have already discussed the prospect of being ambushed by technology, but any kind of aid, cue or presentation tactic has the potential to spring a surprise, how ever well it may have worked in rehearsal.

So you need to plan for problems, and if you have a plan you can implement it – rather than go into panic mode – when you need it. Having a plan to implement also keeps you in the best frame of mind to maintain a brave face as you deal with the problem, ideally so that no one even notices.

Magicians are arguably in the most precarious position of all, being reliant on assistants, stage hands, technicians and props, all of whom need to work together in creating an apparent miracle. As with people, such as the best news presenters, they learn the skill of remaining unruffled when a problem occurs. That, really, is the key to coping when things go wrong. The presenter needs to avoid showing surprise because that can soon turn into mild panic and so interrupt the smooth-running of the presentation.

So how do you apply this approach to business presentations? Consider the situation I once faced when the gremlins decided to attack my DVD player. There is one section in my training programme on Creative Thinking where I address the topic of decision-making. I like to preface this where possible with a short clip from a well-known TV programme that shows people in a meeting arguing about a decision to the point of upsetting each other, rather than reaching any kind of real consensus. It is by no means essential to show this clip, it merely acts as a nice scene-setter and introduces some variation in the format.

As I was about to cue the video clip I looked down at the DVD player, which I had tested before we started, and it was not working. I surreptitiously reached, while speaking, for the switches, but still it failed to come on. Now getting noticeably a little flustered, I apologized to the delegates, saying that I was going to show them a film clip but it didn't seem to be working. I paused for a moment to collect my thoughts and then carried on, albeit with my tail between my legs. Later, amongst generally positive feedback was a comment: "Shame the technology didn't work." What I learned from this was that there was absolutely no need to share with my trainees the fact that the DVD wasn't working; they had not been expecting a DVD clip and would have been none the wiser if I had simply carried on without a mention. I would have been a little frustrated at having to work without my planned enhancement, but they would have been perfectly content and had no little failure to report in the feedback.

So you need to do all you can to minimize the gremlins. Thereafter, boldness of delivery can get you through, possibly without anyone even noticing there was a problem. Just to prove that the gremlins get to even the very best and most prepared speakers, take a look at the video of Steve Jobs unveiling the iPad in 2010. The whole point of the new product was that it was the newest and most satisfying way to interact with the internet. To demonstrate this Jobs went and sat down as if he were relaxing at home or in a café, but he couldn't display anything on the iPad because he couldn't get a WiFi signal.

With such a big news announcement many of the audience were blogging and tweeting direct from the event, overloading the venue's WiFi capacity. Jobs, however, did not panic; he calmly explained that too many people were online and could they please log off for the duration of his demonstration. He used the fact that people were so keen to report the exciting news immediately to overcome what could otherwise have been perceived as a weakness. Such a situation had clearly been anticipated and planned for because at the next break point – as he built up towards a big finale – he was passed a message from backstage about the precise number of people still online. "Do you want to see the final part of the demonstration?" he appealed to the audience. A big positive wave of support came back, putting real pressure (from the audience, not him) on the remaining rogue tweeters to log off. It may be overstating the case to say that he made the problem work to his advantage, but he certainly came close. And the launch was judged a great success.

8.5 The "Starbucks Test"

Finally, having done all you believe you can to prepare for your presentation, ask yourself this question: If I arrived at the venue and they were to announce "Sorry we've double-booked the meeting room / We have a power cut / Whatever, so we're going to do it over the road in Starbucks," how would I fare?

Could you pull off a credible presentation without your aids and a formal meeting space? It's a question worth asking for at least two good reasons. First, it may happen to you one day. I speak from experience on this matter. If it does, you need to make a judgment whether to refuse to present in unreasonable circumstances or whether to battle on. There is no right or wrong answer to this one. Second, if you are prepared enough to present well in such challenging circumstances, just imagine how good you will be with all the proper facilities laid on.

In a nutshell

Give priority to rehearsal – if you're too busy to rehearse, you're too busy to present. Do all you can to make every aspect familiar. This makes you good, helps you overcome nerves and sets you up to cope with problems when they occur.

PART III

DELIVERY

Now comes what is actually the easy bit – provided you have done the work on *Construction* and *Preparation*. As I said at the outset, if you invest time in *Construction,* your *Delivery* will be very much easier because it has a proper structure and flow to it, and you are speaking from the heart so it all comes naturally. The *Preparation* process, meanwhile, will give you the feeling of a safety net when the *Delivery* time comes – you have minimized the chances of anything going wrong and have solutions ready if it does.

Chapter 9
ARRIVAL ROUTINE

Familiarization;
taking control of the space;
positioning yourself

9.1 Familiarization

ALI BONGO WOULD BE COMPLETELY READY FOR HIS SHOW A
FULL TWO HOURS IN ADVANCE OF CURTAIN UP.

The day of the presentation has arrived and you need first to think about your arrival routine. Build in plenty of time to arrive and set up, then add half an hour. That way you will have time to deal with any problems that may occur along the way. It should also leave you some free time when you can get into something approaching a relaxed frame of mind. We all know the feeling of being a bit flustered when starting an important meeting – the traffic was bad, your colleague had to go back for the documents, the promised equipment was not quite as specified and you never had time to have that final run through, let alone check yourself in front of a mirror.

Now imagine the opposite of such an experience and you will be feeling a little like the late Ali Bongo, former president of The Magic Circle, used to feel when preparing for a performance. He would have all his props in place and be dressed in his costume and make-up some two hours before performance time. He would then wander around, chat to people and have a cup of tea so that he felt completely familiar with the whole scenario and the people involved. Remember what I said about overcoming the fear of the unfamiliar? Ali was doing this in the most positive manner, to the extent that he would eventually be getting a little bit bored and therefore be raring to get on with the performance.

One final point about the familiarization process: If there are people working as technical support, get to know their names and befriend them a little. Such people are often overlooked, becoming almost "invisible", and yet you may well be dependent on them to ensure your presentation goes smoothly. If you have taken the trouble to show an interest in them and their work they will be on your side, wanting you to succeed and all the more attentive to the fine details of your needs. And if anything goes wrong during your presentation you can say: "Can we call for Derek (or whatever name) please." While you may be panicking inside, it gives the impression you are still in control and to an extent it transfers responsibility (and blame) to your new friend Derek.

9.2 Taking control of the space

Magicians working as "table hoppers" at banquets – perhaps the most demanding of all performance situations – will not start performing until they have gained everyone's attention, cleared some space for themselves and made an arrangement with the waiters not to interrupt.

Voice check

One of the advantages of arriving nice and early is that there are probably few people around, so use this to your benefit and start by speaking out loud into the room from your designated position. This is a voice check, which you should aim to do whether or not you are using a microphone. The reason is that acoustics can vary enormously from room to room; you may be surprised how much you need to project or boost your volume in what seems an ordinary-sized room. You want to find this out in advance rather than by trial and error at a key moment in your presentation.

From experience I have found that rooms with wood paneling generally have warm acoustics that require little additional effort from the speaker. Places like ships may have a lot of plastic construction so you need to project further towards the back. Marquees need projection and power because there is nothing but cloth to help the sound resonate. Needless to say, talking apparently to yourself comes over as a bit odd, so seize the opportunity for a voice check as soon as possible while there is no one around.

Lighting

Adjust the lighting to suit your needs, drawing any curtains and blinds that are close to your screen (remember the confectionery company at London Zoo) and switch lights on and off to create the mood you require. If you are planning to switch lights on and off during a presentation, say to re-focus from yourself onto a video and then back to you, be very clear which switch controls which light so that you can avoid fumbling around. I usually stick a little piece of Blu-tack onto the light switch I am aiming for.

Layout

Think how to rearrange the furniture to suit your needs best and just get on and do it. If you ask permission they may say no or they may go off to seek approval from a senior person who has better things to worry about. If you just do it, they probably won't mind, may not even notice and the worst that can happen is that you have to apologize for a minor misdemeanour. Just make sure you leave things as you first found them before you depart.

Distractions

You should also eliminate any potential distractions in the area from which you are presenting. Stand back in the room so that you can see your presentation space from the audience's point of view. Is there anything that might distract the audience when you want them focusing on you? If so, can you remove it or cover it? In my early days as a trainer I had a Q&A session before lunch when someone asked me: "What is the mermaid for?" "What mermaid?" I replied. "That one on the wall behind you," came the answer. I had not taken the time to step back and see things as my audience would, so throughout my session they had been constantly distracted from what I was saying by the thought of what I might be about to do with the mermaid.

Owning the space

The best magicians will take time and trouble to create and establish their own performance area before they get started. This is especially apparent with those magicians who do table-hopping performances at banquets. It's a tough environment where a magician has to break in to a table, interrupting the chatter, then create a performance space from nothing in a way that everyone can see, even though many will have their backs to him. So they have strategies for introducing themselves, rearranging a few seating positions, selecting volunteers and claiming a piece of table space for themselves. The more skilled operators will probably do this under the guise of some charming introductory chat, having probably already done a deal with the waiters to avoid untimely interruptions (rather like getting to know the technical support). The point is that they have created attention and space in which their performance stands the best possible chance of being a shining success, despite the challenging circumstances.

Confession time

On a final note about creating your own space, I have an admission to make. Just as I move furniture, I sometimes take out people's light bulbs. The fact is that many office layouts are not well planned. It is quite common to find that you cannot switch off individual lights – it is all or nothing, perhaps for an entire floor, from a switch somewhere outside the room. And occasionally a light is shining directly onto the screen or where I most want to place the screen. So I simply remove the offending light bulb or unscrew it just enough to disconnect it. Needless to say, I always replace such bulbs before leaving, but I doubt I would get a positive response if I asked permission.

9.3 Positioning yourself

MAGICIANS HAVE TRADITIONALLY PERFORMED WITH A "GLAMOROUS ASSISTANT". THE ASSISTANT IS ALWAYS CAREFULLY POSITIONED IN A SUBSIDIARY MANNER SUCH THAT THEY ENHANCE THE MAGICIAN'S PERFORMANCE WITHOUT STEALING ANY LIMELIGHT.

Follow Rules 5 and 6 wherever possible:

- Setting yourself up close to your screen and visual aids, creating a Single Point of Focus.
- Working left-to-right from the audience's point of view (because in most cultures we read that way).

If you have a large space between yourself and the screen – as often happens on conference platforms, mainly because they want to fill the stage in a neat, symmetrical manner – the audience will need to choose whether to focus on you or the screen. And because the screen is big and bright and constantly changing, it is usually going to be the winner. The only alternative for the audience is to move their gaze backwards and forwards, as if watching a tennis match, and they are soon going to tire of that.

Setting yourself up left-to-right can often be something of a challenge, as many establishments have lecterns already installed on the right. Many of the venues at which I have spoken – The British

Library Business Unit, the Royal College of Art lecture theatre and the theatre on board the *Arcadia* cruise ship, for instance – are set up right-to-left. If, however, you carry a gender changer (see Chapter 7.4) and extension leads you can position yourself wherever you want.

Left-to-right is not by any means a hard and fast rule, but it is interesting to observe experienced speakers, especially those who trained as actors, who like to work the stage a bit. Invariably they tend to gravitate towards the left as their home position, even if everything is geared up for right-side positioning. There are actually good reasons sometimes to set yourself up on the right. The BBC's Adam Shaw told me he was concerned, having heard about Rule 6, that the director of his television programme always placed him on the right of the screen. I explained that this was absolutely appropriate in his case as he was reporting on the movement of share prices and the most important part of his screen was on the right – where the share price now stood on a graph that showed movements over time. By standing on the right he was creating a Single Point of Focus in exactly the most appropriate place.

Finally, having positioned yourself close to your screen, be careful not to get so close that you start casting shadows. This is acceptable briefly if you are drawing attention to key points, but if you stay too close you will be inadvertently creating distractions for your audience in the form of hand shadows.

In a nutshell

In order to be on peak form in a presentation you need to own the space. A proper arrival routine sets you up to achieve that.

Chapter 10
ENGAGEMENT

Introductions – framing and supporting each other;
first impressions;
opening

Having created your own space on arrival and seized as much control of the room as you can, you are ready to start.

The *Construction* work you will have put into making this stage work to best effect includes:

- Anticipating the perceptions and associations you are triggering automatically in the minds of your audience (Rule 1) – *Chapter 2.1*
- Considering how you could build on those perceptions – or perhaps play them down – with elements of Prestige, Atmosphere & Environment and Desire (Rule 2) – *Chapter 2.1*
- Building your content around what the audience already knows with familiar reference points (Rule 3) – *Chapter 2.2*
- Making your message important to your audience through elements of personalization (Rule 4) – *Chapter 2.4*
- Scripting and rehearsing your Intro with particular care because firsts and lasts are remembered (Rule 13) – *Chapter 3.2*

10.1 Introductions

Always have someone introduce you. This quietens the room, heightens anticipation and has the potential to create a powerful framework for all that you are about to say. The person introducing you can communicate your best points – and the reasons to listen to you – much more effectively and credibly than you can. If you do it yourself, it just sounds like boasting.

The important thing is to ensure that you do not leave those words of introduction to chance. *You* must provide them to the person making the introduction.

If you leave the words to chance there is potential for them to be either inaccurate or inappropriate. Furthermore, the person introducing you might actually steal your thunder – telling the audience some of the things you have prepared for key moments in your speech, maybe even using one of your best jokes. When I talk about this in my coaching I often find close colleagues saying to each other: "You're always doing that to me!" Team members can play a really valuable role in supporting and building each other up through the way that they interact. It can also be invaluable in projecting the team as cohesively team-like rather than simply people who happen to work in the same place.

10.2 **First impressions**

Much of your *Preparation* has also gone into rehearsing the Intro and Outro (Rule 13 – *Firsts and Lasts*). There is little else you can do at this stage about first impressions, other than to address anything that will inevitably be on the minds of your audience. If, for instance, you happen to have acquired a black eye or a broken arm, then it is important to make a brief mention immediately and then move on. If you make no mention, it will be a constant distraction as your audience wonders about the circumstances of your misfortune rather than focusing on what you have to say.

A magician I used to know was exceptionally rotund in appearance, so he always started his act with the phrase: "I may not be one of the world's best magicians, but I am certainly one of the biggest." It was his way of saying, "OK, I'm fat, now let's focus on the magic," while gaining a little sympathy and support in the process.

So address any burning issues upfront, but make sure the mention is brief – you are seeking to dismiss the potential distraction, not bring it to life.

10.3 **Opening**

Remember that firsts and lasts are remembered (Rule 13), so it is important to stick to your carefully constructed and rehearsed Intro plans. Aside from that, there is really just one more thing to do at this stage and that is to apply a little "hyper confidence".

If you are slightly more energetic or full of beans than feels entirely natural it will help to kickstart your presentation. The audience will feel your energy and it will bounce back off them, reflecting on you. I have seen this so often when coaching business people. The delivery of their business presentation early in the day is often a little flat – they probably feel they are being business-like. But there is no need to be boring just because it is business. I encourage them to use more energy, especially up front. When they return to present their magic trick they apply the energy, partly due to my advice but also because they feel it appropriate to the presentation of a magic trick. You really can feel their energy, which also enlivens their body language and puts a smile on their face that we can hear in their voice. The task then becomes to apply at least some of that approach to their business presentation; if they can do that, the engagement of their audience is assured.

In a nutshell

Firsts and lasts are remembered, so this is one of the two most important parts of your presentation. Your Intro, however, is even more important than your Outro because if you get it right you should sail through thereafter; get it wrong and you will forever be playing catch-up.

Chapter 11
PERSONAL TOOLS OF ENGAGEMENT

*Voice – projection, microphones, variation of pitch, pauses,
"sidebars", umms, errs and bogey words; warming up;
Eyes – using eye contact to engage and direct attention;
Body – standing or seated, stillness, gestures*

11.1 Voice

You need to be heard at the back of the room and have your presence felt there as well, all without deafening those at the front. The answer lies in learning to project – using your breath to support your voice when required. Size of room and its acoustics dictate the need to project, and with luck you will have had the opportunity to gauge the acoustics of the room at a pre-presentation voice check.

In order to project:

- Imagine that your voice originates in your abdomen or lower back rather than your throat.
- Inhale.
- As you exhale, let your breath carry the sound.

If you are in a convenient place try it now. Announce yourself to an imaginary audience first without the breath, then with the breath. You will see immediately that the latter version is certainly a little louder, but more importantly, it adds depth, resonance and presence.

With a little experience you will soon find yourself shifting into projection mode automatically when required. There are, however, two points to remember. The first is control; you don't want to project unless it is actually required; we all know certain people who appear to have their "project button" switched on almost permanently and their company can become quite tiring. Second, your degree of projection really needs to be synchronized with your eye contact – the personal tool I discuss next. You need to be heard clearly by the entire audience throughout your talk, but as your gaze reaches the back it is fitting that your voice should match your gaze and reach full projection; similarly the level of vocal projection can fall back a little as your gaze scans those nearer the front.

Microphones

The need to project becomes less of an issue when you are using a microphone, but should not be discounted altogether. While a microphone should make you audible throughout the room, you still need to reach out to the audience as a whole and that needs a degree of projection.

With regard to the choice of microphone types, defer to the sound engineer unless you have a compelling reason to use one type or another. Magicians, for instance, tend to need their hands, so often prefer a lapel mic, but some actually use the mic stand as a prop and may also need a hand-held to make their volunteers audible.

Lapel mics are generally easier to use because you just speak as normal; in fact you soon forget you are even wearing a mic, which points to the one danger area when using a lapel mic – forgetting to switch them off (at the battery pack fixed to your waist) when your presentation finishes. We have all experienced or heard stories of unguarded backstage comments or even the flushing of toilets being broadcast loud and clear because someone has forgotten to switch off their lapel mic. Nowadays in the UK we have a shorthand warning for this: *Don't do a Gordon Brown!* The former British Prime Minister was already in deep trouble during the General Election campaign of 2010 when he left a media walkabout without removing his mic. The session had not gone well, and as soon as he was in his car he made a derogatory remark to his aides about a member of the public who had confronted him. The comments were caught on tape and broadcast repeatedly over the coming days, raising serious questions about Brown and his suitability as a leader. No party won the election outright but there was little doubt after that incident that Gordon Brown would lose.

When using any kind of mic do not concern yourself with volume – that is the responsibility of the sound engineer. You do have to help them, however, when speaking into a hand-held or a mic on a stand by keeping a consistent distance. So don't stoop towards the mic or keep adjusting it; adjust it initially if required and leave it to the soundman thereafter. If using a hand-held you will need to adopt a rather stiff-arm posture to maintain a consistent distance.

Variation of pitch

Having found the right level of projection, you need to apply movement and change in order to retain the audience's attention. This is Rule 11 again –

> Attention is sustained by variation, which shortens mental time.

I discussed Rule 11 at the *Construction* stage and talked of "chunking up" the content in order to bring the variation that sustains attention. Exactly the same applies with the voice: keep it all at one (monotone) level and attention will drift away; introduce variation and you have a much better chance of retaining attention. The deeper breathing I discussed for projection gets you off to a good start in bringing vocal variation. Thereafter:

- "Lean" on important words and phrases, putting a little more energy into those particular words, for example: *Lean on important words and phrases, putting a little more energy into those particular words.*
- Inject emotion into key elements – display your excitement in appropriate places.
- Emphasize the ends of statements and questions, for example: *Emphasize the ends of statements and questions. Do you understand what I am saying?*

Break any obvious patterns. For example, I would generally advise against reading out lists, but if you have a need to do so, stop after a few points and make a brief comment on one; then continue.

Pauses

Using pauses is one of the most powerful ways of adding impact through variation. Start by speaking a little slower than in normal conversation and then build in a pause wherever you want to add dramatic interest. In particular, add a pause where you need to highlight a really important point. The pause does the highlighting for you and then allows the point to sink in properly.

Winston Churchill was the master of the pause. After the Fall of France in 1940 he wrote the following speech:

> Let us therefore brace ourselves to our duties, and so bear ourselves that, if the British Empire and its Commonwealth last for a thousand years, men will say, "This was their finest hour."

This, however, was no ordinary speech; it needed to be the most powerful rallying call the British people had heard in generations, so he delivered it as follows, with six pauses built in:

Let us therefore brace ourselves to our duties	PAUSE
and so bear ourselves	PAUSE
that if the British Empire and its Commonwealth	PAUSE
last for a thousand years,	PAUSE
men will say,	PAUSE
"This	PAUSE
was their finest hour."	

Each pause created focus around a key aspect of the speech.

You simply don't hear oratory like that these days; or do you? This is how Steve Jobs announced Apple's introduction of the iPhone:

In 2001 we introduced the first iPod.	PAUSE
It didn't just change the way we all listen to music; it changed the entire music industry.	PAUSE
Well, today we're introducing three revolutionary products of this class. The first one	PAUSE
is a wide-screen iPod with touch controls. The Second	PAUSE
is a revolutionary mobile phone.	PAUSE

And the third   PAUSE

is a breakthrough internet communications device.   PAUSE

[...]

*These are not three separate devices. This is one
device*   PAUSE

and we are calling it iPhone   PAUSE

Today Apple is going to re-invent the phone.

By pausing in this manner Jobs built up a rhythm which started to create its own applause cues; he soon had to pause – in order to take the applause.

Sidebars

One of the best places to change your tone a little is as you relate an anecdote. This immediately signifies that you are taking a slight break from the normal run of commentary and, as you are telling a story, a slightly warmer, quieter and even tone may be very appropriate. As you change tone again after the end of your story this too signifies that you are back into the main narrative. It works rather like a sidebar in a newspaper or magazine. A small illustrative story, some deeper detail or perhaps an amusing coincidence, may be separated from the main story in a boxed section, so breaking up a solid block of print, making the layout more attractive and easier to read.

Umms, errs and bogey words

We all do it – pepper our speech with a series of umms, errs and other sounds that are often specific to us individually. In everyday speech these do little harm, indeed they perform a specific function that the linguists refer to a "voiced pauses". They fill gaps in the conversation and create thinking time and break-in points. Less acceptable are "bogey" words such as "you know", "kinda", "like", "literally" and "sort of", many of which follow the latest fashion in slang. As a result, they particularly affect the young, who simply soak them up, tending to be unaware they are even saying them.

There is a lovely example on YouTube where my young broadcaster friend, Matt Edmondson, a former member of The Young Magicians Club, has edited an entire TV documentary on C-list celebrity Peaches Geldof, leaving only the bits where she says: "like". You will be amazed – as I am sure she herself was – that it still makes a lengthy clip; you can find it by searching for "Peaches Geldof – master of the English language." At around the same time in the USA Caroline Kennedy was expressing interest in standing for the Senate seat vacated by Hillary Clinton. The dream of continuing the famous political dynasty was soon dashed, however, as her media performances became the subject of ridicule. An interview in which she said: "you know" more than 35 times in two minutes was one of the last appearances she made before withdrawing her name.

So while bogey words should always be avoided, umms and errs are acceptable to a degree in everyday conversation. None of them, however, have any role in presentations or any kind of more formal communication, where they become much more noticeable, increasingly irritating and serve to de-emphasize whatever you are saying.

You will need help from a friend or colleague to identify and iron out your bogey words – probably on an on-going basis as new ones are soaked up. The answer to avoiding umms and errs is a simple one and it comes back to good scripting and enough rehearsal to *know what you are going to say*. The reason umms and errs have no place in presentation is that their role as voiced pauses is to fill conversation gaps, create break-in points and thinking time. The first two of those are immediately redundant because you don't need thinking time if you know what you are going to say, especially if you have a Confidence Card as back up.

Remember that, aside from de-emphasizing what you say, umms, errs and bogey words are irritating; even if you can handle the de-emphasis, you certainly don't want to irritate. Which brings me to a final bogey factor – the upward inflection, which has become increasingly common, even among the older generation, and thereby increasingly irritating. The upward inflection occurs when the speaker raises the tone of their voice towards the end of a sentence as if asking a question. This is appropriate if you *are* asking a question as in "Shall we go for a drink *tonight?*" but completely misplaced in a straight statement of fact such as: "I went for a drink last *night.*"

As with bogey words, people tend to adopt the upward inflection by simple absorption. It needs to be avoided because, irritation aside, it gives the impression that you are unsure of yourself and are being tentative in your statements. An upward inflection indicates a suggestion from which you can readily backtrack if you receive a poor response; so, again, it undermines what you are saying. If you are seeking to convince, watch out for the upward inflection.

Warming up

Finally, bear in mind that, just as your legs need warming up before you run, your voice and mouth need similar preparation if they are to function at their best on what is effectively an extended vocal workout. This is particularly so if you are presenting early in the morning; you simply cannot expect your voice to get up to speed in terms of tone, diction and flow from a standing start.

A good way to warm up your voice is as follows:

- Hum a tune with your lips shut.
- Do the same with your mouth open.
- Speak a series of tongue twisters out loud. This will prove just how below par your mouth can be without a proper warm up.
- Then speak your opening lines in a range of different styles and accents.

Meanwhile, drink plenty of water and definitely have some close by while you are presenting. But keep it very securely – we all knock our drinks over from time to time and you are all the more likely to do so when your energy levels are pumped up.

The last thing to do before you start presenting is a simple breathing exercise:

- Inhale three layers of breath without exhaling.
- Then exhale slowly through the mouth for longer than inhalation.
- Repeat twice.

11.2 **Eyes**

"IF YOU WANT SOMEONE TO LOOK AT SOMETHING, LOOK AT IT YOURSELF. IF YOU WANT SOMEONE TO LOOK AT YOU, LOOK AT THEM."

THE MASTER OF DIRECTING ATTENTION,
MAGICIAN JOHN RAMSAY

So much of our communication seems to come from the voice that it is all too easy to overlook the importance of the eyes. Eye contact is essential to true engagement – it positions you as more credible, trustworthy, confident and assertive, as well as more friendly. The American mind-reader, Marc Salem, highlights the power of eye contact by pointing to the huge variations we can achieve by communicating with eyes alone: *blank stare; wink; glare; downcast look; laughing look; if looks could kill, she looked daggers at him; bedroom eyes.*

If you have any doubt about the importance of eye contact, the moment you have children and have to teach them to say: "Thank you for having me," you realize that it simply won't work without accompanying eye contact. Similarly, as we grow up, we realize that handshakes and saying "cheers" over a drink are relatively empty gestures unless matched with eye contact.

Eye contact, nevertheless, needs to be worked at, partly because many people may feel uncomfortable – initially at least – with such close personal contact. Depending on the size of your audience, you need to look at members individually, holding eye contact for just a little longer than might feel comfortable. Often this will generate a response such as a nod or a smile, so you know they are engaged. Eye contact then needs to be spread, not mechanically so, but ensuring that everyone in the room is receiving equal attention.

With larger audiences, where you can't actually see directly into their eyes, you need to adopt a similar approach but scan across different groups. And if you find yourself in a theatre-style situation with a lot of lighting on you, you will see virtually nothing in front of you. This can be very un-nerving so, as part of your familiarization process, ask to stand on the stage with the lighting as it will be for your presentation. Then you have to mimic the eye contact and its movement because, while you can't see the audience, they can certainly see you; and whoever happens to be in your eyeline will wonder why you are staring at them. That said, there may well be an option of having some of the house lights switched on during your talk – you should enquire about this if you feel more comfortable presenting that way.

Many people I have trained admit they have given little thought in the past to eye contact, and one even came to the realization that he was lucky to have secured his current job. Thinking back, it dawned on him that his final interview was with the ultimate boss, who was flanked by two decision-making lieutenants. He gave the majority of eye contact to the boss, at the risk of making the lieutenants feel quite left out. On other occasions, I have described this scenario and had people relating stories of being in the position of those lieutenants and perceiving the interviewee much less favourably than the boss who again was receiving the majority of the eye contact.

Magicians arguably know more about the importance and benefits of eye contact than almost anyone else because they use their eyes to direct attention. Now, it has to be said that there is often subterfuge at play when magicians use their eyes to direct attention. When they have your gaze caught in theirs they can be up to no good with their hands and props elsewhere. This, of course, is *mis*-direction and, while I would never encourage anyone to use the deceptive side of magic to advantage in business, there is still plenty we can learn from magicians.

Spanish magician Juan Tamariz recommends using imaginary strings, as follows:

- Pretend that strings connect your eyes to the eyes of each audience member. Keep the strings tight – by returning their gaze – and don't allow the strings to sag, or they will break.
- If a string breaks work quickly to re-tie it. Walk towards the inattentive person. Move back to others only when you have the defector back on board.
- Locate key people and focus on them.
- Check the eye colours of audience members – to force close eye contact.

Matching eyes to body language
Finally, I started this section by highlighting the importance of the eyes as a means of communication. It is useful to remember the old

proverb: "The eyes are the window to the soul." In other words, the eyes reveal our true feelings, displaying whatever we are really feeling inside. This is most evident when it comes to the smile – you can fake the mouth part but unless joy can also be seen in the eyes the overall effect will look forced and fake, resulting in what used to be known as the "Pan Am smile", because it was common among American flight attendants. Remember that for communication to be effective you need to convince as well as engage.

11.3 Body

Standing or seated?

Your first decision is whether to sit or stand – there is no right or wrong on this. Standing allows you to be more expressive, but sitting can be useful in restricting the movement of those who fidget around too much. I would advise considering two factors. First, what feels most comfortable to you; second, gauge the mood of the meeting. Might it feel a little odd to stand when everyone else is sitting? Alternatively, might you be expected to stand as part of the procedure of making a presentation? There is, of course, a third option which can be highly effective as long as it looks impromptu: stand for the main body of the presentation, then join everyone sitting at the table when it all moves into a more conversational mode. Your move to a seated position can in itself signal a change of gear.

Stillness

There is much that movement can do to add impact to your communication, but before you can deploy gestures to good effect you need first to learn how to keep still. While too much movement can create distractions and make the audience work, stillness helps to create focus. Actors talk about the power of stillness, and even the most energetic magicians use contrasting stillness to bring focus at the moments when attention is most vital. If, for instance, you watch

Paul Daniels on YouTube presenting his signature "chop cup" routine you will see a performance that is described as fast and furious. By the time he comes to the climax, however, he is absolutely still, with his feet fixed very firmly to the ground.

The trouble is that many people – myself included – find it difficult to keep still, particularly when our energy is pumping at full throttle, so we need to work at keeping still. Steve Cohen, who bills himself as the Millionaire's Magician and can be seen at his long-running Chamber Magic shows in New York City, has good advice on keeping still. "If you stand with both feet pointing forwards," he says, "weight will naturally shift from foot to foot and you will rock like a boat. The audience won't be able to focus properly and you will look nervous and uncomfortable." He therefore advocates the "45-degree rule", whereby you keep your right foot pointed forward and place your left heel to the back of the right heel at a 45-degree angle. That way you are firmly anchored to the spot. If you look again at Paul Daniels' chop cup routine you will notice that, as he reaches his climax and comes to a still position, his heels are together, with feet at a perfect 45 degrees.

The game changes a bit when you find yourself on a large stage and you need to fill that space. If you are using a screen, the slides can do much to help you in that respect. It is in the moments that you have a break from the slides – and possibly at the beginning and end – that you should consider coming out from your home position and working the stage a bit. What you want to avoid is too much striding around or moving backwards and forwards in a fidgety manner.

Again, there is a problem with role models here in that people see comedians careering around all over the stage and start to believe that freeform movement is the way to go. British comic Michael McIntyre, for instance, famously goes from side to side with a hop and a skip that has become a trademark. While I am not going to suggest that comedians' stage moves are as carefully planned and timed as their script, I would say that their movement is part of a personality that has been carefully crafted and honed over hundreds of gigs, with analysis opportunities coming through instant live feedback and hours of TV coverage. And, just as certain top sportsmen have a combination of skill and peculiar traits that enable them to break traditional rules with success, so do some top stage performers. The rest of us do so at our peril.

Having introduced some movement and worked the stage at appropriate moments, you should come back to your home position (ideally on the left from the audience's view) and stay still when you need to focus attention very specifically. If you watch Steve Jobs at his product launches, he wanders the stage in the introductory phases, welcoming his audience and soaking up the applause. He might continue this through a few scene-setting slides, but by the time he wants you to focus on the detail or see the new product he is back in home position on the left of the stage.

Gestures

Having learned how to achieve stillness – though realistically you will probably find this is a matter of work in progress – you can consider how judicious use of gestures can add impact to your presentational style. Remember how important the visual sense is to taking in and then retaining information? Here is the opportunity to put that into practice by reinforcing your words with complementary gestures such as:

- nodding – as you say yes
- open handed – to underpin openness
- hands expanding – to express growth and development
- hands contracting – to express coming together
- clenched fist – to express determination
- on the one hand, or the other hand – to compare alternatives
- smile – to express pleasure

As with Words That Paint Pictures, the audience can now see what you are saying as well as hear it. Ideally this should come naturally. The more you become relaxed as a presenter and true to your own style, the more you will find gestures do come naturally. So start by paying closer attention to the gestures you are using as a matter of course and then consider how your key points might be appropriately amplified with additional gestures.

Whatever you decide, you need to be conscious of your gestures – natural or planned – because it is essential that they match, or at least do not conflict with, what you are saying. Aside from the sort of people who fail to convey excitement as they talk about supposedly feeling excited, I have seen people actually shake their heads from side to side as they say "yes". Just as the visual sense can add significant power to what you are saying, it can also overpower your words if it appears to conflict with them.

So, having said earlier that video is not necessarily always helpful as a tool for presenters, it can be very useful for ironing out any discrepancies or identifying annoying gestures that – like bogey words – the presenter may be unaware of. Some people, for instance, simply don't know what to do with their hands and adopt a strange pose as a result. One person I coached held his hands up to his chest and then flat, throughout his presentation. I was distracted by the thought that he must be getting uncomfortable. Another person constantly twirled his right arm around from the elbow. Neither of them were the slightest bit conscious of these inadvertent poses, but the arm twirler recognized his as the way that he danced. The best time to use video is once the basics have been achieved and you are looking to iron out small details, such as I have discussed here.

The answer to what to do with your hands, by the way, is to keep them slightly together in a relaxed arms-length manner. This prevents too much fidgeting and provides a home position from which to make effective gestures. That said, if you are using a slide changer – and if you are using slides you really *should* use a slide changer – that gives you something to do with your hands and the problem tends to go away.

In a nutshell

Become aware of how powerful your personal tools of engagement can be and you will soon be using those tools instinctively, to great effect.

Chapter 12

TECHNICAL TOOLS OF ENGAGEMENT

PowerPoint – making it support you as a presenter;
slide changers; pointers; video clips

12.1 PowerPoint – making it support you as a presenter

Having considered the personal tools of engagement, we come to the technical tools of engagement, and PowerPoint in particular. The tools are ranked in this order because, as I said earlier, *you* are the show, PowerPoint has a supporting role at most.

With this thought in mind, you should aim to establish yourself before letting any visual aids potentially compete for attention. It could be a good move, therefore, to start without the Powerpoint presentation showing.

You will often see magicians and other performers start and finish in this way. They may have a big supporting cast and an array of props, but they like to establish themselves upfront and also to close with a quiet personal moment between themselves and the audience. It's Rule 13 about firsts and lasts again. Remember that in business, whatever you have to sell, in most cases it is *people* that the customer is ultimately buying.

Keep looking forwards

Most people understand that it is bad practice to simply read out your slides, but many seem to have missed the fact that you shouldn't really even look at your screen. PowerPoint should not be a substitute for notes – it is clarification for the audience, not a crutch for the speaker. The problem is that, for a variety of reasons, many people find they simply cannot help looking at their screen and doing so continually as though they have never seen their slides before. The result is that their voice projects in the wrong direction, the vital element of eye contact goes out the window and the audience just gets a nice view of their presenter's shoulder.

Aids, such as Apple's *Presenter Tools* (see Chapter 8.3), help the presenter to know where they are and what is coming next, while maintaining eye contact with their audience. So make sure you have a laptop or monitor in front of you. If it is not equipped with *Presenter Tools* keep a simple note of the slide titles and their running order.

Magicians and actors have a horror of "backs to the audience" instilled into them, but it's not just a question of vanity; maintaining eye contact is absolutely key to directing attention and creating impact. The only time you ever *do* want to look at your screen is to direct attention there specifically, so think of weather forecasters again – set up left-to-right, using the back of their hand to point, and looking into the screen only to draw attention to key points.

12.2 **Discovering the lights under PowerPoint's bushel**

In Chapter 6 "Uncovering the lights that hide under PowerPoint's bushel" was listed as the second of three principles you need to understand in order to achieve "Powerful PowerPoint" – presentations that actively support you as a presenter. Here we look at some of the tools that are offered by PowerPoint, but remain undiscovered by many presenters.

Clearing the screen

As I touched on briefly in Chapter 6, the B button is probably the archetypal light that remains largely hidden under PowerPoint's bushel.

- If you press the B button when projecting PowerPoint it will blank out the screen. Press B again and the slide reappears.

This makes it one of the most useful tools for a presenter as it helps to bring attention back to the speaker, reaffirming that they are in control. It breaks the trance that can set in with PowerPoint, as it shifts the focus from technology to people.

- The W button performs the same function but whites out the screen rather than blanking it. Press W again and it brings the slide back.
- Many remote slide changers also have a blanking function.

The ability to clear the screen is extremely useful in terms of directing attention, but consider also what happens if you don't blank the screen. You only want the screen to display support material for what you are discussing at this moment. If you leave up an image relating to what you were talking about 10 minutes ago it is going to act as a constant, on-going distraction.

I saw the perfect example of the need for the B button when attending a credentials presentation from a leading PR consultancy. Towards the end – at a very appropriate moment – the presenter said: "Let me tell you briefly about some of the fun things we do – we have girls' nights out. [Up goes a slide of a group of young women enjoying such an evening.] We find this a great way of reaching and developing relationships with some of our key targets, many of whom are young single women." After a little more detail his tone of voice shifted noticeably as he announced: "So, why should you appoint us? Three reasons, first ..." In many ways it was a model presentation, but we weren't really paying attention to what he was now saying at the most crucial moment because we were still looking at pretty girls on the screen. Had he used the B button, he would have cleared a distraction out of the way, brought attention back to himself for his most important concluding messages and flagged up the change in tone.

The B and W buttons are also useful, of course, if you wish to open and close without PowerPoint, as I discussed at the beginning of the chapter.

Flexibility

Here we can tackle two of PowerPoint's Seven Deadly Sins – No.2 *Makes the format rigid* and No.5 *Kills the art of business conversation* – head on.

You sometimes see the audience in a business presentation itching to focus on one particular aspect that is probably coming up later in the presentation by asking questions about it now. The trouble is that when they are using PowerPoint, presenters think their hands are tied and they end up making a plea: "Please bear with me – that is coming up" – in about 26 slides time!

- **Jump to facility**

  As it happens, you can jump to any point in a presentation that you wish, provided that you have a note of the slide numbers. You simply key in the number of the required slide, press return and your computer moves seamlessly to that slide. Do bear in mind, though, that if you wish to return to where you were, you need a note of that slide number too.

  You need to use your judgment to decide whether to let your audience dictate the running order. But remember, you are seeking to create empathy and to match what you have to say with what they want to hear, so in the right circumstances the most effective route can be to cut straight to the chase and focus on their favourite topic. Indeed, my most memorable training sessions have been the ones where discussion has developed so effectively that the PowerPoint presentation has become superfluous, so I close it down (or hit the B button and leave it).

- **Hyperlinks**
Hyperlinks offer a formalized, pre-planned version of the jump to facility. In this case you can build in a hidden link on a specific slide that will take you directly to another slide of your choosing. This gives you flexibility and the additional benefit of openness.

   I encourage companies, such as marketing agencies, to use hyperlinks when showing case histories as part of a credentials presentation. The usual routine is to show a list of clients, probably in the form of a group of logos, and then run through a series of case histories for some of those clients. This technique can be made significantly more powerful if you show a group of client logos and then invite your audience to select which they would like to hear about. It works juke-box style – you click on that logo and PowerPoint takes you straight to that case history; at the end of the case history another hidden hyperlink returns you to the juke box selection point.

   The advantages are that the audience members don't have to sit through stories which don't interest them; they feel they are in control and the agency comes across as very open, as if saying, "Ask me anything you like, feel free to speak to any one of our clients." In reality, of course, the agency has limited the selection available, just as a magician will probably be limiting the selection of playing cards available as he says: "Pick any card, any one you want."

   To use the hyperlink facility click on "Insert" when in PowerPoint, then click "Hyperlink" at the bottom of the drop-down options and follow the instructions. Watch out, though, for colour schemes; once you have clicked on a hyperlink in a presentation the font changes colour to indicate you have used it. As PowerPoint is always so helpful in suggesting formats and so on, it will pick a colour for you; you may well want to change this to something less garish.

Writing on your slides

PowerPoint even offers you the option to write in freehand on top of your slides, maybe to add arrows or additional elements to existing slides, or even create something new on a blank slide. To activate this facility you click on the pen shape in the bottom left-hand corner of PowerPoint while it is in Slideshow mode and this offers you a menu of pen types, including highlighters, colours and thicknesses.

I personally would avoid using this facility unless you have had plenty of practice. It is hard to draw accurately using a mouse pad, and other, more user-friendly options that enable you to use a pen-like instrument are emerging all the time. If you need to do a lot of drawing, for instance for brainstorming, these items of new technology are worth investigating. One advantage is to be able to save your work on a computer while facing the audience throughout.

One way in which you could use PowerPoint's own drawing facility to good effect is by preparing your freehand drawings in advance. Say you have a slide with a range of 10 options and you really want to persuade your audience to pick two. You could copy that slide and draw rings around your chosen two or crosses through the eight you want them to ignore. You then show the first slide and discuss the 10 options before moving on to the copy that shows your recommendations in vivid style, as if you had just drawn on that first slide.

12.3 **Slide changers**

Use a slide changer whenever you can and ideally use your own so that you are completely familiar and comfortable with it.

The reason you need a slide changer is that, while you should generally keep still, you don't want to be tethered to your laptop and you don't want to have to reach for a button every time you change slide, nor risk hitting the wrong one.

Changing slides should be like changing gear in a car, in that you can soon do it without looking down or even thinking about it. So go for a changer that sits snugly in the hand and can be manipulated very easily and accurately by feel alone. Sadly some of the most modern changers have put style over substance and you can achieve neither of these important needs very easily.

A good slide changer should also have – probably alongside vibrating timers that I find a little superfluous – a blanking button, so that you don't even need to reach for the laptop's B button, and a laser pointer.

12.4 **Pointers**

I am not a great fan of laser pointers, mainly because even the steadiest hand cannot keep them still on the screen and you end up with a little coloured dot dancing around the spot you are seeking to highlight. I prefer to be more hands on, literally, and use my hand to point to the desired spot. If this creates a bit of shadow on the screen for a moment, no matter; it brings me and the item on display together. In certain situations, however, the screen is simply too big or too high for you to reach so you have no choice but to use a pointer if you need to highlight a specific point.

You might like to ask yourself why it needs such special highlighting; is your slide perhaps too cluttered? Undoubtedly, though, there are occasions that you do need a pointer, so it's best to have one that's built in to your slide changer, meaning one less item to handle, clutter your space and run out of battery power. It you have a choice, though, go for a pointer that projects green, as this is proven to show up more clearly than the more common red.

12.5 **Video clips**

Murphy's Law again – *If it can go wrong, it will go wrong* – is more true than ever when it comes to showing video clips. How many times have you seen the video elements of a presentation fail to start; start after a series of glitches; start in the wrong place; start without either sound or vision; or start at the wrong volume? What is meant to enhance, clarify and illuminate your presentation undermines it, with the result that the sense of momentum and pace is lost, along with your own confidence.

For these reasons my advice at the *Preparation* stage in Chapter 7.4 included:

* Use your own equipment wherever possible.
* Use separate machines for PowerPoint and DVD.
* Be in control of the equipment yourself if possible.

So, in an ideal world you would operate as follows:

* Laptop and portable DVD player are in front of you, with the DVD paused in the correct starting place (visible from DVD's screen display). Remember that a sleep function often over-rides the pause function after a while, so switch to pause as close to play time as possible.

Smooth switching from PowerPoint to DVD and back is then a simple process of:

* Switching the source button on the projector or TV screen's remote control from Computer to AV.
* Swiftly followed by switching the DVD to play.
* Pause DVD to stop.
* Switch screen remote to Computer to bring back PowerPoint.

- Turn the DVD off (or you might find that it continues with sound only).

If the video clips must be controlled by a technical assistant, for instance in a theatre set up, then deal with that technician yourself and:

- Agree clear cue-in and cue-out points, both verbally and in a written brief.
- Provide DVDs with clearly marked chapters, ideally with the chapter that starts just ahead of your cue-in points.
- Preferably give them only what they actually need, that is, if you are playing a short clip, give them a DVD with only that clip, thereby eliminating the danger of playing the wrong clip or failing to find it or cue it correctly.
- Remember to retrieve your DVD before you leave.

Video clips should, almost by definition, be brief. Don't feel you have to run them all the way to the end – they can all too easily slow down the whole pace of a presentation, rather than provide some sparky movement and change. Just as you should sense the mood of the audience as you speak and edit yourself down or expand according to reactions, so the same should apply to video clips. The ideal clip should have a series of potential cut-off points so that you can keep it short, if that appears to fit the mood, or let it run if they are clearly enjoying it. Again, this is another good reason to be in control of your equipment if possible.

You may find it appropriate to provide some commentary as the video clip plays. If so, you need to decide in advance whether to simply talk over the video's sound, pause the video or turn the video sound down as you come to speak. The answer will depend on a number of factors, such as sound levels on the video and the room you are in, and it may be dictated by whether or not you are in control. If you are making very brief comments – which is generally best – the simplest solution is probably to talk over the video. But you don't want to end up with a mush of sound where nothing can be heard properly.

In a nutshell

Remember that they are tools and treat them as such, picking your favourites, using them only when required and putting their most useful features to work for you.

Chapter 13
DIRECTING ATTENTION

Creating focus; re-directing focus;
using visual aids; eye contact killers

The *Construction* work you will have put in to make this stage work to best effect includes:

- Establishing clearly defined objectives, complete with action points – *Chapter 3.1*
- Applying high focus to the points you most want the audience to remember (Rule 5) – *Chapter 3.1*
- Tailoring your approach to suit this specific audience (Rule 4) – *Chapters 2.3 & 2.4*
- Chunking up your content to sustain interest through variation (Rule 11) – *Chapter 3.4*
- Editing your content – killing some darlings along the way – to ensure that every element is supporting your key messages and actively moving the story forward (Rule 10) – *Chapter 4.5*

13.1 Creating focus

IF THE MAGIC HAPPENS IN A FLASH THE MAGICIAN NEEDS ATTENTION TO BE IN THE RIGHT PLACE AT THE RIGHT TIME OR EVERYTHING IS MEANINGLESS.

You can only direct attention properly once you have mastered the art of eye contact and, as I discussed in Chapter 11.2, this is an area where magicians have a distinct advantage. If your eye contact is strong, the audience will follow your eyes and look:

- where you look
- where you point
- where you tell them to look

It has to be said, however, that they are even more likely to look in the following places:

- wherever there is movement, sound or contrast
- wherever there is anything new or different

When I explain these last points in my training courses, most of the audience are immediately distracted and look around to the back of the room because they have heard a cat crying in the corner. This is, of course, a sound effect that I have triggered by remote control, but it proves the point and shows how the factors that seize and hold attention can be both your friends and your foes.

So you need to keep as much control as you can over the attention grabbers with three specific tactics:

1. Plan and assign audience positions so that their gaze falls naturally on the speakers and their aids, and away from potential distractions, such as activity through windows or glass partitions.
2. Eliminate distractions wherever possible. I have already discussed clearing away anything that might catch the audience's eyes while you are presenting, but think also about impromptu distractions. The classic example is the arrival of coffee.

   How many times have you or a colleague just launched into a presentation and the coffee arrives? You simply cannot hope to compete – at one of the most crucial moments – with the clinkety-clink of cups and saucers and whispers of "Would you

like sugar with that?" So stop – and make a point of stopping
– by helping serve the coffee, thereby speeding the process and
remaining in control.

Magicians are well experienced in this area because they
usually have to handle a few latecomers, many of whom will be
looking for seats near the front. The best magicians will have
tried and tested ways of handling this, whether it be with witty
lines or simply by building in a prologue element at the front
that helps to establish a relationship with the audience while
also improving the chances that latecomers will have arrived by
the time they get around to doing anything important.

3. When distractions do occur unavoidably – such as the siren
   of a passing ambulance or police car – again, don't try to
   compete with it; pause for a moment, together with a brief
   witty phrase if you can think of one, and then continue once
   the distraction has passed. If there is an on-going distraction,
   such as builders drilling, you probably need to resort to a
   form of bribery that encourages a change of schedule or an
   early tea break.

   In certain situations you may need to *re*-gain focus, and
   here a couple of very eminent magicians have some useful
   advice. When addressing an audience that includes one or
   more coughers, Derren Brown advises the presenter to speak
   more *quietly*. The instinct, he says, is to speak louder, but by
   going quieter it forces the audience to listen harder and it puts
   pressure on the cougher. As for talkers, David Berglas advises
   moving towards audience members who are talking, without
   looking at them specifically. If they continue to talk, he says
   rather pointedly: "Can you hear me at the back?" On receiving a
   positive response, he looks directly at the talkers, saying: "Good.
   I can hear you too."

13.2 **Re-directing focus**

ONLY BY HAVING A STRONG HOLD ON THE AUDIENCE'S ATTENTION FROM THE OUTSET CAN THE MAGICIAN THEN DIRECT ATTENTION TO WHERE HE NEEDS IT TO FOCUS.

At certain points you will want to re-direct attention, either because the time has come to move on to a new topic or because you are seeking to build in elements of movement and change (Rule 11) that shorten mental time, so helping to retain attention.

We have already discussed how variation in the pitch and tone of your voice can help to re-direct focus, especially in instances such as deploying anecdotes as illustration. There are also a number of more physical options for re-directing attention and these include:

- Coming out from behind your lectern, closer to the audience, for a more intimate moment.
- Leaning forward – in a small meeting this signifies that you want to come closer to your audience to underpin a point that you need them to *feel* as well as understand.
- Lowering the voice – if done briefly this can have the same effect as the techniques above; it brings the audience towards you by forcing them to listen harder.

Another tactic you can use is the simple ploy of flagging up the fact that you are about to say something important or significant. Two very different British personalities use exactly this technique, which I therefore call the Blair/Daniels Technique.

- Former Prime Minister Tony Blair often prefaces a point he really wants to get across with: "I think the really important thing is …"

- Similarly, the UK's most famous TV magician Paul Daniels will trail the big moment in a trick with: "Now watch this, because this is going to be incredible ..."

In each case they are drawing in attention at a key moment, so framing up their big message. Importantly, eye contact will be used in conjunction with the Blair/Daniels Technique. In both cases the eye contact will become that little bit more intense as they make their spoken plea for attention, and Daniels' gaze will then turn to whatever he is asking us to watch.

Finally, remember to keep clearing the screen, using the B or W buttons. You don't want to be forever switching the screen image on and off, but you only want to use the screen when it is supporting what you are saying at this moment.

13.3 Using visual aids

VISUAL AIDS – OR PROPS – CAN MAKE OR BREAK A MAGICIAN'S PERFORMANCE. AT BEST, THE PROPS AND THEIR DEPLOYMENT ENHANCE WHAT THE MAGICIAN IS DOING; AT WORST, THEY CONFUSE AN AUDIENCE AND STEAL ATTENTION FROM THE MAGICIAN.

During the *Construction* and *Preparation* stages you will have:

- Planned aids that truly support what you are saying as well as introducing variation – *Chapter 4.6*
- Ensured that your aids are scaled to suit the size of your audience – *Chapter 4.6*
- Used thickness of line rather than scale to ensure visibility – *Chapter 4.6*
- Planned the handling of your aids – where you are going to keep them and then put them away – *Chapter 8.2*

The simple rule of three for visual aids at the *Delivery* stage is:

1. Display them clearly – steady, straight and close to your body.
2. Linger for a while – rather longer than seems natural.
3. Put them away – unless intended as a lingering image.

What tends to happen is that people go to the trouble of bringing a visual aid, keeping it close to hand for the right moment. Then they waste that time and effort by making such a cursory display of the item – too quick and held at an awkward angle – that the audience feels frustrated rather than enlightened. There is nothing worse than a visual aid that does not aid the audience.

Another common scenario is that the presenter manages to display the aid successfully, but then leaves it on display, creating an on-going distraction. Remember my trainee who failed to focus our attention on his closing points because he had left up the slide of the girls' nights out? Generally speaking, you need to clear each aid away, but there are exceptions to this rule. Your presentation might be about gradually building an overall picture, in which case leaving the aids strategically placed around the room could be very effective – as long as you have planned this carefully.

More likely, there may be a case for using a lingering image that sets the tone for the whole presentation or leaves the audience with a thought to take away. By their nature, lingering images are usually best deployed at the beginning or the end. A variation on this theme is to use the image as a "full circle" rather than lingering device. Here you would introduce the image at the outset so as to set the tone for the presentation; clear it away during the presentation; then produce it again at the end, to bring the audience full circle to where you started.

Some of the magic tricks I ask delegates at my training days to present involve a number of cards bearing a series of different words and images. These are usually tailored to their company or organization, but the main objective behind the tricks is to train the delegates in the handling of visual aids. Holding up a bunch of cards sounds so easy and yet they soon realize, first, how clumsy you can become when under pressure and, second, the fine line between making a visual aid work for you and having it cause confusion.

Having displayed your visual aids, be wary of passing them around. This may seem a natural, friendly and helpful thing to do, but the main result is that you progressively lose the attention of each audience member as it goes around, especially if they feel the urge to whisper comments to each other. It's generally much better to display the item and invite them to come up and see it for themselves at the end. That way you keep everyone's attention and can move on to the next point. Also, effort is not wasted on those who do not feel a need to examine the item.

Graphs and charts

With graphs and charts you need to take a moment to help your audience orientate themselves with the axes, the key, the scale displayed and the time period or other details. Only then will they be able to properly appreciate the point you are seeking to make with the graph.

What tends to happen is that presenters launch straight into their point, with the result that the audience is bombarded with a lot of visual information at once and can find it hard to even see the key element that the presenter is pointing to, let alone fully appreciate its significance. The ideal situation is to present a first slide that simply shows the axes, so that the audience understands – without the opportunity to jump ahead – the layout and scale of the graph. This leaves them well primed to then take on board the key points as the data is overlaid on a second slide.

This step-approach can be especially useful when showing comparative graphs of, say, growth of a company's revenue over time compared with the market as a whole. What people tend to do is to put the whole graph – with one line for the company and another for the market as a whole – up at once. Aside from hitting the audience with too much information, this approach completely throws away the opportunity to tell a great story, drawing the audience in as that story unfolds. If you have a great story to tell, then don't spoil it by giving away the ending up front. Think about how you can spin the story out – milk it, if you like – along these lines:

- Put up the basic graph showing only the market as a whole.
- Explain the axes, for example, revenue up one axis and a 10-year period along the other.
- Tell the story of how the overall market has evolved over the years, in as much detail as is required but aiming to keep it brief.
- Then add in the line for your company, but in small chunks of a few years at a time, telling the story as you go and relating back to relevant points you have made about the market overall. For example, "This was when the recession kicked in," (pointing to a downward turn for the market overall); then introduce the next part of your company's performance (showing, hopefully, an upward inflection).
- Having demonstrated a pattern of outperforming the market, you can then create some tension around whether you have been able to sustain that performance.
- Unveil the final portion of your company's performance to satisfy their intrigue and complete the picture.

It all comes back to a Single Point of Focus, in this case creating a series of Single *Points* of Focus so as to add to your overall impact.

13.4 **Eye contact killers**

MAGICIANS WILL NEVER BREAK EYE CONTACT UNTIL THEY
WANT THE AUDIENCE TO LOOK SOMEWHERE SPECIFIC.

The importance of eye contact should by now be self-apparent – it
really is the key to directing attention. So what happens in a situation
where everyone expects to work through a document? Heads are
down, the document is the focal point, and attention can wander all
over it – probably to the all-important concluding ideas and numbers
that form your proposed climax.

Working through a document continues to be the expected
norm in certain industries, especially those that need to focus on
complex sets of data. I was particularly struck by this when working
with people in the financial sector. I would watch some PowerPoint
presentations and gradually coax the presenters into strengthening
their eye contact. Then we would move on to a presentation from a
document and everything I had just said about eye contact seemed
to become redundant.

If your audience expects to work through a document, you need
a very compelling reason to deny them this expectation. So I worked
with my clients in the financial sector to develop a method of having
it both ways:

- Communicate your key points *before* handing out the document
  – as a kind of extended introduction. This way you have full eye
  contact, distractions are avoided and you are in control of the
  agenda.
- Having essentially made your presentation in a top-
  line manner, you then hand out the document *to discuss
  supporting detail*.
- Retain control even at this stage by telling your audience where
  to look. For example, "I am going to hand out the documents

now and ask you to turn straight to page 5, where you will
see …" Having asserted yourself upfront they should follow,
especially if it clearly links to what has just been discussed.
Keep this up: "Next, please look at the first column on page 8,
where …" until you have made your key points and are happy
for it to lapse into general discussion.

Finally, remember to take charge again at the end so that you can
sum up and send the audience away with your key points.

In a nutshell

While your mindset should be a strong feeling of "being in charge
and telling the audience what to do", you should be able to achieve
this without anyone being properly aware.

Chapter 14

IMPACT ISSUES

*Eliminating distractions in the wider environment;
identifying the "nodding off" point;
handling questions; the placement of questions and your climax*

The *Construction* and *Preparation* work you will have put in to make this stage work to best effect includes:

- Planning the layout and focal points – *Chapter 7.2*
- Detailed planning and plotting to ensure you really know what you are going to say – *Chapter 4.1*
- Identifying the points and words that need special emphasis and clarity – *Chapter 8.2*
- Building in Words That Paint Pictures so that your audience can "see" what you are saying as well as hear it – *Chapter 4.3*
- Changing weak words into strong words – *Chapter 4.3*
- Turning negatives into positives – *Chapter 4.4*
- Engaging as many of the five senses as possible – *Chapter 2.5*

A number of issues then need to be considered to ensure your presentation creates as much impact as possible.

14.1 Eliminating distractions in the wider environment

Rule 9 – The wider environment can often add to or detract from your message

We talked in the Arrival Routine section (Chapter 9) about removing distractions in the immediate environment – avoiding situations such as having a mermaid steal attention from you as you present. But what of the wider environment? Can you do anything about all the other issues that may be on the minds of the audience, potentially distracting them from your presentation?

If you know that something is inevitably on their minds you should do all you can to factor it into your communication. Alastair Campbell, who was head of communications for British Prime Minister Tony Blair, was the master in this area. Just like a magician, he took the view that everything had the potential to either add to what he was seeking to communicate or to detract from it. He used a news management system known as "The Grid" onto which he plotted all the government announcements he was planning for the coming weeks. Then he added national events such as major sporting fixtures and items that would feature prominently in the popular media.

So if, for instance, the England football team was playing a big match the night before an important government announcement, he planned that announcement in the knowledge that a significant proportion of the population and the media could well be in a state of either euphoria or deep gloom as his news broke. If a pop star was appearing in court on, say, a driving charge, it just may be that this would coincide with an announcement by the Home Secretary. If so, the two stories could well be combined; would this help or hinder the government's story and should Campbell consider advising the Home Secretary to delay or bring forward his announcement?

Applying this principle to business presentations, consider what might be on the minds of your audience at the time of your presentation. Then factor it into your communication.

• Is the person a big fan of a particular tennis player who has now made it through to the quarter-finals at Wimbledon on that very afternoon? If so, offer to either re-schedule or start and finish the meeting early, with the promise of a meeting room with large screen to watch the match at his leisure.

• Have you heard that they have a particular need to catch a specific train in order to reach another important meeting? If so, start the meeting with travel arrangements as the first item on the agenda; invite them to look through the window to see a car that is already waiting for them and tell them that you intend to conclude 10 minutes earlier than scheduled, just in case of traffic problems.

Do whatever you can to eliminate anything that has the potential to distract your audience from your message. I was running a training day for a major car manufacturer one day when news started coming through that a major redundancy programme and part-closure of one of their factories was about to be announced. It soon became apparent that, inevitably, their minds were elsewhere. So rather than simply battle on, I suggested that we take a break for a full hour and re-evaluate things then. They were grateful that I was showing empathy and had taken the initiative to suggest something they would soon have demanded. They went away, made as many calls as they could and all returned within about 25 minutes. They realized there was little they could do but wait and the training day was actually a good opportunity to take their minds off it all. As far as possible, I had eliminated the distraction.

14.2 Identifying the "nodding off" point

How ever good you are, there will come a point in almost any presentation that can be identified as the "nodding off point". It usually comes about three-quarters of the way through, where the audience is well attuned to you and nicely relaxed in their seats. See if you can do something that nudges them out of that comfort zone and sharpens their attention ahead of the final wake-up call you will give them just prior to your climax.

Among the ploys I use at the nodding off point are:

- Making an outrageous suggestion – so as to deliberately stoke up argument and debate.
- Switching off the PowerPoint and changing to a completely different form of media.
- Looking for inspiration from the movie world, with the display and discussion of a range of movie posters – something that they weren't quite expecting at that point.

Such tactics work a bit like the point in a dinner party when the host suggests everybody changes places; the guests all see the party from a fresh new perspective and it takes on a whole new energy.

14.3 Handling questions

As with so much good presentation practice, much of the most important work here should happen in advance – anticipating likely questions and rehearsing answers, probably in fairly broad categories, as we discussed in Chapter 8.2.

Difficult questions should therefore not be too difficult if you have been through rigorous rehearsal. When it comes to *Delivery* it is important to remember that, while you don't have to directly address difficult questions, you do have to acknowledge them or they will turn into a running sore. As with questions of any kind, you should seek to match what you want to say with the questions the audience is asking. With a difficult question this match may be less close than for other questions. Having acknowledged the question, however, you are justified in moving on to other people's enquiries.

Before answering any question, pause for a moment. This buys you a little time to consider the answer (or remember what you have rehearsed) and indicates a considered response.

If you don't know the answer it is usually best to admit as much and promise to come back with an answer. Alternatively, you can throw the question open to members of the audience, one of whom may have the answer. This appears very open and it can also be a good way to reduce the heat when you get difficult questions. So, seek alternative views from amongst the audience, provided that you can keep them under fairly strict control.

Finally, you need to be convincing as well as accommodating and efficient when answering questions. A useful tip here is to make a few notes as you go. It's easy, for instance, to say: "I'll come back to you on that," but it is far more convincing and therefore powerful to be seen to be making a note of whom you need to respond to, on what. That shows commitment.

14.4 The placement of Q&As and your climax

It might seem like a small matter, but where you place a Question & Answer session within your presentation could be crucial to its impact and success. The reason for this is that most people assume Q&As come at the end – that seems the natural place and that's the way it has always been done. I urge people, wherever possible, to consider the placement of their Q&A carefully and do things a little differently.

My general recommendation is to place the Q&A session slightly before the end, so that you keep your climax under your control. Remember Rule 13 – *Firsts and lasts are remembered*. If you place Q&As at the very end, it may be that someone asks a really insightful question, you give a brilliant answer and the audience members leave with that ringing in their ears. That, however, is leaving it very much to chance; it's much more likely that some misfit at the back finally gets to have his say and brings everything down to his level.

Or perhaps no one asks a question. Everyone goes away with the memory of an embarrassing silence. Here you should step in to fill the silence with a Frequently Asked Question along the lines of: "Something I am often asked is …" as we discussed at the *Preparation* stage in Chapter 8.2.

You want to send your audience away with a clear climax that embodies your key message. So my general recommendation is as follows:

- Just before your conclusion say: "Before I conclude, what questions would you like to ask?"
- You answer a few questions and state that you have time for one more.
- You answer that and then say: "Thank you for your questions, now to conclude …"
- You hit them with your pre-prepared climax that contains your key messages, including a call to action.

It is, if you like, the real world equivalent of the "ta-dah" moment at the climax of a magic trick. Much of what a magician does is about building up to the moment at the end that the audience is going to go away and talk about, so you want as much focus and attention around that moment as possible.

This point is highlighted very clearly by some of the magic tricks that I get my trainees to present. It may be that the ta-dah moment is created by the opening of an envelope to reveal whether or not a prediction is correct. Here, the presenter has to decide whether he is going to open that envelope himself (potentially less convincing) or allow his audience volunteer to do so (appearing very open). If the presenter has chosen his volunteer carefully he or she *may* react with great enthusiasm, announce the result in a good, clear voice and hold it up close to her face so that everybody can see it, but that's leaving a great deal to chance. She may simply mumble the answer, put it back in the envelope and, feeling a little self-conscious, turn to speak with her friend. Not much of a climax. If, however, you allow your volunteer to play an active part earlier on when focus and timing are less crucial, a degree of openness and audience involvement has been established. You can then open the envelope yourself, staying in control of the big climactic moment at the end that the audience is going to remember.

I once attended the launch of an academic book in a university lecture theatre. The author was a visiting professor and he made a presentation, concluding with a Q&A session. Realizing he was running out of time he called for "one final question", only to find that it came from another member of the university with whom he did not see eye-to-eye. As expected, the question was neither friendly, nor helpful, let alone suitable as a conclusion to the event. The author handled the question as well and as swiftly as he could (acknowledging it but not really addressing it) and said: "Actually we do have just enough time for one more." He scanned the room in search of a friendly face, found one and ended the event on a positive note. On hearing my advice about placement of questions when I lectured his students a couple of weeks later he commented, with a wry smile, that he would employ this tactic next time he gave a presentation.

In a nutshell

The power of your presentation can be magnified, or reduced, squashed even, by aspects that remain largely hidden.

Chapter 15

DELIVERING YOUR CLIMAX AND CONVINCING YOUR AUDIENCE

15.1 **Your climax**

Having planned to ensure that you are in control of your climax, all you really need to do at the *Delivery* stage is to implement your climax strategy and be bold about doing so. Bear in mind also, that if you are using PowerPoint you may want to finish without it – using the B or W button to blank the screen – so that full attention comes back to you.

- Start by **signposting the end**, with a simple statement such as "As I draw to a close ..." This refocuses attention at a point where many of the audience will have become just a little too comfortable, how ever engaging they find the speaker.
- Then **reiterate your key messages** loud and clear in a way that is familiar and yet fresh. Essentially this will be a summary – and therefore a repeat – of the key points, but see if you can find a different way to frame it, ideally in a way that brings yourself and your audience together.

  In my training sessions, for instance, I often conclude by laying out a grid of squares on the screen. The background of the squares is in the colours of the company or organization I am visiting and the first of 12 squares feature their logo. The remaining squares are then gradually filled with reminders of key points I have made during the day, so these are now sitting in a collection, blended with the client's corporate identity. I ask for a volunteer and lend them my magic wand; I request that they make some random moves around the grid while I look away, after which I will attempt to read their mind to determine where they have ended up. Needless to say, they always end up on the most important square of all – their logo!

- Mind reading that logo creates the final element required for an effective climax – an **applause cue**. You don't usually expect applause when giving a business presentation, but you still need to make the end absolutely definite. If the audience is saying or thinking "Is that it?" you have failed; you need a combination of tone, rhythm and body language that indicate you have reached your conclusion.

15.2 Convincing your audience

Again, much of the work needed here will have been done at the *Construction* stage (see Chapter 5) with special focus on:

- Self-conviction
- Being yourself
- Openness and accidental convincers
- Avoiding "un-convincers"
- Being wary of switching to "auto-pilot"
- Self-confidence

Conviction will then be strengthened during the *Preparation* process (Chapter 8), which should have included:

- Three-stage rehearsal
- High focus on the Intro and Outro
- Prompt aids
- Planning for questions

When it comes to *Delivery* there are really two main factors to consider, and you already have these covered as well:

- **Knowing what you are going to say.** As I said up front, if there is one, albeit ridiculously simple, secret to successful presentation, this is it. Knowing what you are going to say, thereby being clear, concise and smooth, makes you both look and feel confident and convincing.

- **Eye contact.** It's all in the eyes – they are the window to your soul. If you are not giving good eye contact you are not going to convince your audience. But you are on very safe ground here because you will have already worked hard at developing your eye contact so as to persuade and direct attention. The good news is that conviction is then thrown in for free.

In a nutshell

Your final opportunity to persuade your audience to do whatever your presentation has been about. So, construct and prepare this more carefully than anything else. Then deliver it from the heart.

Chapter 16
INSPIRATION FROM THE WORLD OF MUSIC

I find it useful to look outside my own immediate world and experience for inspiration, and there is one standout example that took me many years to fully appreciate. I particularly like it because it embraces what I see as the three essentials for successful presentation – and you can see many of the Rules of Magic at play.

The supreme example for me is Queen's performance at Sir Bob Geldof's Live Aid concert in 1985. Sir Bob echoed the thoughts of many around the world when he said: "Queen were absolutely the best band of the day." I believe they achieved that feat by focusing in equal measure on *Construction, Preparation* and *Delivery.*

Many bands rested on the laurels of past glories and seemed to think about little more than *Delivery*, with the result that some – such as Led Zeppelin – struggled. Bob Dylan was notable for busking it – and ruining a high point as a result – and Dire Straits were quoted as saying that they happened to be playing in the adjacent Wembley Arena so they simply wandered across the car park with their guitars.

Queen, meanwhile, went into planning mode, starting with *Construction*:

- What needs adjusting, bearing in mind we are not playing to our own audience? Solution: we will build on what they already know (Rule 3) with a greatest-hits package.
- How much time have we got? A: 20 minutes. Solution: Edit our hits into a medley, which will also shorten mental time. (Rule 11)
- Strategy for ending (Rule 13): *We Are the Champions* as a sing-along statement song.
- Clear objectives (Rule 5): Steal the show.

So, much careful thought went into the *Construction* of Queen's appearance, but it was only when I got to know Lesley-Ann Jones, author of *Freddie Mercury: The Definitive Biography* that I discovered another part of the plan that led to the band's Live Aid success. In terms of *Preparation*, Queen spent a full week rehearsing for their set at London's Shaw Theatre. And, having created a perfect 20 minutes, they honed it down to 18 minutes to give themselves a little leeway. The result – "Queen were absolutely the best band of the day."

As it happens, there was also a little bit of magic in the way that Sir Bob Geldof secured Queen's agreement to play at Live Aid. On the day of the concert his ranting and raving style of cajoling people's involvement and contributions reached its peak, but his approach to Queen was altogether more calm and considered. He had heard that Freddie Mercury had always been adamant that Queen should not involve themselves in anything that could be interpreted as political, so he was warned that it would almost certainly be a "no" from Freddie. Armed with this information, Sir Bob adjusted his normal "People are dying – you've got to help" spiel. Instead he said to Mercury: "You've got the whole world as your audience Freddie, Queen were *born* to do this show." Freddie immediately warmed to the idea of the whole world as his audience and agreed to do the show.

Appendix

1. The key differences between Conversation and Presentation

In Chapter 4.2 we discussed the need to keep your language both conversational and plain English in style. You want to avoid sounding stilted, and if your choice of words is overly formal it will hinder your attempts to engage your audience. There are, however, important, albeit subtle, differences between a conversation you would have with one or two people informally and a presentation you give, even if you are only addressing a small audience.

What sets Presentation apart from Conversation is partly the need for high focus on what you are saying. Above all, though, it is the pure practicality of the fact that with Presentation the communication is predominantly one-way, with little or no opportunity to butt in and ask for clarification. You can't, for instance, turn back a page to check a point as you could if you were reading a book. Consequently, Presentation needs to be:

- **More direct** than day-to-day conversation. When we looked at the danger of negatives in Chapter 4.4, I commented that the British are more prone than many others to show reserve, but most of us hold back a little on our viewpoints in conversation so that we can feel our way in, gauging the standpoint of the person we are speaking with and then elaborating, clarifying and perhaps modifying our own viewpoint accordingly. There are no such needs or opportunities in presentation, so you should be rather more vociferous and adamant – outspoken even – than you would expect to be in a more relaxed one-to-one communication.

Strong Words and Avoiding Negatives are two of the techniques previously discussed (Chapter 4.3) that help to make presentation style more direct.

- **Shorter and punchier** than day-to-day conversation. While Conversation has its ebbs and flows, complete with umms and errs as punctuation, Presentation needs to be concise – you must know what you are going to say. Don't be misled by conversation that you see in drama. This is *dialogue* rather than conversation and it is largely unreal as it has been edited of all the meanderings and superfluous words that you would hear if you were to record a genuine conversation.

Placing the most important words at the front of a sentence and using active verbs (see Chapter 4.3) makes communication shorter and punchier.

- **Packed with clarification.** There is no room for even a hint of ambiguity in Presentation. As I have said, there is no opportunity to re-read a point you have just made, so important points need all the enunciation and pauses that we have discussed in order to let them register. Also, words that might fall into clarity traps need to be spelt out, sometimes literally, for example: *Sales are down to 15 per cent of their original levels; that's one – five*, (in case anyone anticipating a higher figure mis-heard it as 50 per cent). As part of the clarification process, feel free to build in repetition, and for key points don't even worry about making that repetition stealthy.

Words That Paint Pictures (see Chapter 4.3) can be used to add clarification.

For presentation, therefore, you need to imagine yourself setting the controls for conversational style, then turning each one up a few notches. This should not conflict with the other essential of being yourself. Comedian Jack Dee talks about how he came to recognize the need to develop a stage persona. That persona, he says, *should be a heightened version of yourself.* The additional benefit, he goes on to say, is that once you have developed that persona it starts writing its own material.

2.   Message distillation techniques

"IF YOU CAN'T WRITE YOUR IDEA FOR A MOVIE ON THE BACK OF A BUSINESS CARD, YOU AIN'T GOT A MOVIE."

MOVIE MOGUL SAM GOLDWYN

Chapter 3 looked at the importance of creating a Single Point of Focus and deciding what you most want your audience to remember. For inspiration we looked at the brilliance of Steve Jobs in coining an SSM (Single Simple Message) that runs throughout his presentations and automatically triggers memories of further details.

I was addressing a group of communication directors from all over Europe one day and found myself following non-executive director Mary Francis, who held a number of very senior positions, including directorships of British Gas and the Bank of England. Her advice that day was: "To make your message understandable you must be able to communicate it in a few short sentences. If you can't, you probably don't understand it yourself." This set me up beautifully for the coaching I was planning on Message Distillation and I sought Mary's permission to quote her alongside Sam Goldwyn, whose words appear at the head of this chapter, and Steven Spielberg, whom we shall come to in a moment.

I offer two forms of message distillation: *Elevator Messages* and *Superlatives*:

i. Elevator Messages

Elevator messages are exactly what they say on the tin – they are concise enough that someone can understand *who you are; what you are;* and *what you can do for me,* in the time it takes to ride in an elevator. If your message is about a product or service it would sum up *what it is* and *what it can do for me.*

The process for creating an Elevator Message is as follows:

- Write down every one of the key words or phrases that sum you up – ideally on Post-it notes.
- Rank those words and phrases in order of importance. One way to do this is to divide them into three categories: *1. Must know; 2. Should know; 3. Nice to know.*
- Eliminate all but the most vital until you have a manageable Elevator Message.
- Develop top-line detail that expands directly from your Elevator Message.
- Experiment with your Elevator Message and adapt as appropriate.

I have used this technique on many occasions with clients and I applied it to defining my own offering when I moved into the training field, as follows:

- **Write down every one of the words or phrases that sum you up – ideally on Post-it notes.**

Training • communications consultant • magic • rules of magic • presentation skills • creative thinking • coaching • for the business community • Client list • Member of The Magic Circle • Member of Chartered Institute of Public Relations (CIPR) • Directing attention • Persuading & Convincing

- **Rank those words in order of importance. One way to do this is to divide them into three categories:** *1) Must know; 2) Should know; and 3) Nice to know.*

Must know	Should know	Nice to know
Training	Coaching	The Magic Circle
Presentation Skills	Client list	CIPR
Magic / Rules of Magic	Communication consultant	PR Officer to The Magic Circle
For the business community	Directing attention	
Creative Thinking	Persuading & convincing	

- **Eliminate all but the most vital – until you have a manageable Elevator Message.**

Resultant Elevator message: *I apply the Rules of Magic to business communication.*

- **Develop top-line detail that expands directly from your Elevator Message.**

I apply the Rules of Magic to business communication. >>>>

A. I specialize in Presentation Skills and Creative Thinking, combining my experience as a communications consultant with techniques I have identified since developing an interest in magic.
B. I discovered that many of the techniques used instinctively by the best magicians for directing attention, persuading and convincing can be extremely effective in the business arena.

C. As well as being an active member of the Chartered Institute of Public Relations, I am a member of The Magic Circle, the world's most prestigious magic club, for which I act as public relations officer.

With the above, I can expand my communication for as long as the elevator ride lasts, but even if I am traveling just one floor, the nub of the message has been communicated; everything that follows is simply supporting detail, the most important of which comes first.

- **Experiment with your Elevator Message and adapt as appropriate**

Over time I gave less emphasis to the Creative Thinking side so as to strengthen the focus. In line with this, I made less mention of my PR background, partly because this was closely linked with the Creative Thinking and partly because I found it less necessary as I became established in my new role.

ii. Superlatives

Superlatives are essentially your "claims to fame" and probably appear in written form – such as in a credentials section at the back of the document for a presentation – so you can be rather more boastful.

The technique here is to imagine that you are appearing on a TV chat show and the host needs to introduce you, devoting around 15 seconds to ensuring that the viewers will stay tuned for the next 15 minutes.

Write a mini-CV and then tailor it to the audience you are addressing and the amount of time and space you have available. I, for instance have a standard 500 words written about myself and I edit this down to around 100 to suit anything from conference organizers, to PR consultancies, to industry organizations, to financial institutions. This is where "basing your communication on what they already know" really comes into play, so drop names shamelessly and the more famous the better.

Drawing inspiration from the movie makers

These techniques probably look quite simple and they are; actually putting it all into practice, however, tends to be rather difficult. I draw inspiration from the movie makers because they have a particular need to distil their messages. They have to start by pitching their idea to the money men – we have already heard what Sam Goldwyn has to say about the need for snappy pitches. Once their film has been made, promotion has traditionally been dependent on the limited medium of posters and word of mouth – they need to get people talking about their movie. Furthermore, the window of opportunity is short. Unless people respond to the word of mouth in the next week or so it will be too late; the movie will already have gone from the cinemas.

Movie makers therefore work around the principle of "High Concept" – a short sentence that tells you all you need to know about the movie and inspires you to go and see it. Examples include:

- An asteroid as big as Texas is hurtling towards Earth – *Armageddon*
- Boy and girl from rival gangs fall in love in the middle of a gang war – *Romeo & Juliet/West Side Story*
- Giant shark terrorizes holiday resort – *Jaws*

My own favourite example of High Concept concerns Sandra Bullock's early success, *Speed*, which was all about: *A bomb on a bus that would go off if the bus travelled at less than 55. And rush hour had just started.* This was really a little too wordy for a High Concept, so within the business it soon became referred to as *Diehard on a bus*. Now you know exactly what to expect.

As Steven Spielberg says: "I like ideas you can hold in your hand. If a person can tell me the idea in 25 words or less, it's going to make a pretty good movie."

Finally, the ultimate High Concept film has to be *Snakes on a Plane*. The High Concept wording stuck for a while as a working title until Samuel L Jackson's agent insisted that a "proper" title be adopted, because his client "couldn't work on a film with such a title." When Jackson heard about this he responded with the much-cited comment: "We're totally changing that back. That's the only reason I took the job: I read the title."

3. "White Cheating"

Whenever I explain to people that I apply the Rules of Magic to business communication I am always acutely aware that my own Rule 1 comes into play – the notion is automatically going to spark perceptions and associations about magicians, and I am hoping they are up to speed with the more cutting-edge exponents, such as Derren Brown as well as the cuddly uncle figures they remember from their childhood. It's very likely also that mention of magic will trigger thoughts of deception and sleight of hand, so I am quick to explain that for business I focus exclusively on directing attention, rather than mis-direction or any form of subterfuge.

All that said, there are times when a little cheating can add real impact without doing any harm at all. I call this "white cheating" because it is like white lies – it's meant for good and it's perfectly harmless because the absolute truth is immaterial.

To give you an example, Tony Blair's former head of communications Alastair Campbell now makes his living in various ways, including speaking engagements. In late 2010 I found myself as a fellow speaker with Campbell at a conference in Nottingham. He spoke very openly about his time at 10 Downing Street and some of the assignments he has taken since, before delivering a motivational piece to his audience of business people. This was based on 10 lessons he learned while at Number10 and which he believes could be usefully applied in the outside world. He introduced it all by relating how he had returned to Downing Street earlier that year to help with the General Election campaign; while doing so he had a final clear out of his old office and came across his list of "10 lessons", which he held up briefly to show the audience.

Now, it may be that Campbell really had written down those 10 lessons on one small piece of paper some six or more years earlier while at Downing Street; it may also be that he left it behind and only retrieved it earlier that year. Whether this actually did happen is immaterial. By framing the talk as he did he added impact in several ways. In particular, he made it more current and it came over as "direct from the centre of power" rather than merely as subsequent reflections on his time in the hot seat. So if I had been advising Campbell, and he had not had a piece of paper to retrieve during the election campaign, I would have suggested that he construct an introduction along those lines.

We have already touched on some of the ways in which a little white cheating can be used to good effect:

Making a story current

Many of the examples I use in my training come directly from watching the people I have been coaching or from attending presentations of all kinds when I am speaking at conferences, so the bank of stories grows all the time. If the time frame is important to the story I will stick to hard facts, but generally speaking a good story about presentation skills is a good story whenever it happened. My audience doesn't care if it happened six years ago and it may sound rather dated if I say as much. So, typically I will say: "I was coaching someone recently and ..." even

if in reality it was six years ago; no one gets hurt. Think back to the old-time comedians who would often start a story with "A funny thing happened to me on the way to the theatre tonight ..." These stories worked because they were current and it felt like a shared experience; a story based around a funny thing that happened to them on the way to the theatre around 18 months ago may be a very good story, but it is simply not going to have the same impact.

Props and prompts

Quoting directly from the source can, as discussed in Chapter 8.3, be an effective way of both prompting you as a presenter and convincing the audience of the quote's authenticity. You may, however, need to mock up the source. I still have the school report that I quote from, but it's getting tatty and I will soon need to "recreate" it.

I also made mention in Chapter 8.3 of the experienced speakers who have no need for notes but nevertheless hold and shuffle some cue cards in case the audience should think they have not bothered to prepare anything specially. These people are "cheating", but doing so for the benefit of their audience.

Making a story universal

Here's a direct confession to "white cheating" from me. In Chapter 9.2 I talked of removing any potential distractions from the area in which you are presenting and I related how I fell foul of a picture of a mermaid. This is completely true except that it was actually a picture of a Chinese woman rather than a mermaid. I changed it to a mermaid so that I could use the story (with an accompanying visual on PowerPoint) wherever I was, without fear of finding I was telling the story to a Chinese woman, who just might take minor offence. One thing I can be absolutely sure of is that I am never going to be confronted by a mermaid. Small adjustments do no harm and can sometimes give you a lot more flexibility.

Questions

Throwing out questions that are likely to gain the "right" answer is a technique we discussed in Chapter 3.3 for gaining attention initially, and that would fall under the banner of White Cheating. As would planting questions, which you might do in order to raise points that you particularly want to make, but it can also be helpful to the audience in that it starts a flow of questions which they can join, rather than making them feel uncomfortable having to go first.

"Impromptu" ideas

One of the advantages of working without PowerPoint is that you have much greater flexibility to chop and change your presentation according to the mood of the audience. It also means you have the opportunity to re-frame carefully constructed material as apparently "impromptu" ideas worked out on the spot in response to comments from your audience. The advantage here is that your presentation comes over as very specifically tailored and your audience feels actively involved and closely in tune with you as the presenter. Thinking back to the use of flipcharts discussed in Chapter 2.6, this is where some near-invisible pencil marks on the flipchart pad can help you to illustrate those apparently impromptu ideas.

Research

I am going to risk the wrath of magicians for a moment and disclose the fact that some mind-reading acts depend on a mix of a little technology and a lot of brass neck. They "reveal" all sorts of facts about the person they are entertaining, apparently by reading their mind, when in fact they have gleaned most of it from Facebook and various internet search engines.

Think about how you might use this technique in a business context. Simply doing the research and playing it back to the person you are presenting to is unlikely to win you many plaudits, even though you are talking about their favourite subject. At worst, you might come over as a little bit of a stalker. Subtle use of personal information can, however, be extremely useful as a short cut to developing empathy. Being aware of their dislikes helps to steer you away from potential danger areas and knowing what turns them on allows you to introduce themes and ideas along the lines of "I feel you're the sort of person who [appropriate comment] so I am going to recommend …" If done sparingly the audience can only be impressed with how much you seem to be on their wave length. Is this cheating? Or thorough preparation?

Finally, for anyone who is really interested in applying the deception side of magic in the real world, I can point them to two magicians who lived double lives. John Mulholland worked for the CIA and Jasper Maskelyne was hired by British Intelligence services to add the art of illusion to the war effort during World War II. Their adventures are recounted in books such as *The MagiCIAn: John Mulholland's Secret Life* by Ben Robinson; *The Official CIA Manual of Trickery & Deception*; and *The War Magician – The True Story of Jasper Maskelyne* by J David Fisher.

4.   **Presentation Magic at a Glance**

The following charts show the 21 progressive building blocks to a winning presentation in terms of the Top 10 Tips for *Construction, Preparation* and *Delivery.*

Top 10 Tips for Construction

1. **Script your intro** precisely – stating your objectives succinctly and engagingly. With a good start you should sail through; a bad start means constant "catch up".
2. **Speak your words out loud** when scripting – writing for the ear is different to writing for the page.
3. Use the pronoun **"you"** frequently. It makes the audience feel included, important, the focus of attention.
4. **Add impact with strong words,** for example, *problems, manageable* and *think* are all weak words that can be strengthened: *challenges, achievable, believe.*
5. Add impact with **Words That Paint Pictures** so the audience can "see" what you are saying as well as hear it.
6. Add impact with **Positives** rather than negatives. Negatives need unscrambling, for example, "Hold it steady" rather than "Don't drop it."
7. In PowerPoint a slide generally makes a **lousy handout** and a handout makes a **lousy slide.**
8. **One-line bullet points** have the greatest impact. Keep font sizes to **24pt minimum.**
9. **Thickness of line** is more important for visibility than sheer scale.
10. **Script your Outro** precisely with:
    a) a fresh reiteration of your key messages
    b) a clear climax and
    c) an applause cue.

Construction

Perceptions & associations
you are triggering in the minds of
this audience
Ch 2.1

Elements of **Prestige, Atmosphere
& Environment, and Desire** to
build on those perceptions / play
them down
Ch 2.1

Familiar reference points
for this audience
Adjustments required
Ch 2.2

Most appropriate
presentation approach
Ch 2.5

Clarity of objectives
with call to action
SSM – Single Simple Message
Ch 3.1

Attention Gainer
Ch 3.3

Chunking – to retain attention
Power of 3
Ch 3.4

Climax
• Key messages reiterated **Ch 3.5**
• Applause cue

PowerPoint
• Take control – map it out
  visually
• Think prime uses
• Structure: Destination **Ch 6**
  > Starting Point > Roads & Bridges
• Scripting – minimum words for
  screen
• Visuals
• Consistency

Ch 5
Conviction
• Self-conviction
• Openness – accidental convincers
• Un-convincers
• Rule 19

Ch 4.7
Differentiation device

Ch 4.6
Visual Aids – use for:
• Visual queries
• Clarification
• Mass of detail
• Similes & metaphors
• Brightening slides

Think:
• Scale
• Thickness of line
• Killing darling aids

Ch 4
Scripting checklist
✓ For the ear
✓ Strong words
✓ Words That Paint Pictures
✓ Positive language

Top 10 Tips for Preparation

1. Tackle **nerves** upfront – the fear of the unfamiliar is the greatest cause of stage-fright-type nerves, so make the scenario familiar to yourself. Whenever possible **see the venue** in advance.
2. When rehearsing, **replicate the scenario** as closely as possible: *layout; equipment; props; likely questions, time of day, dress*. This identifies gremlins and makes the situation familiar.
3. Speak a little **slower** (about 120 wpm) than in regular conversation (about 170 wpm). Work at achieving this and build in pauses to force it if necessary.
4. Rehearse your **Intro and Outro** more than anything else.
5. Brief the person handing over to you how you want to be introduced. Then rehearse **introductions** and handovers.
6. Keep **technology simple** – it can ambush you. And avoid relying on third parties wherever possible.
7. Keep **prompt notes** small and stiff and confine them to a simple **map** that gets you back on track with a glance if needed.
8. With PowerPoint aim to use **Presenter Tools** whenever possible – its display shows: *slide projecting, run of slides, next slide, notes area* and *clock/timer*.
9. **Time** your rehearsals carefully and aim to come in a little under time. The brain plays tricks on you and it will invariably seem longer or shorter than it really is.
10. **Stop** rehearsing **24 hours in advance** whenever possible – allowing clear thinking and time to visualize both the process and doing it successfully.

Preparation

Pre-production

Checklist
- ✓ Who and how many are you seeing?
- ✓ Where are you seeing them?
  – venue visit
- ✓ How long do you have?

Equipment **Ch 7**
- ✓ Screens & positioning
- ✓ Own equipment where possible; technical liaison where not
- ✓ Extension leads and tape
- ✓ Gender changer
- ✓ Table at speaking position
- ✓ What can go wrong?
  – plan your outs

Rehearsal

Replicate the scenario
- ✓ Layout
- ✓ Technology
- ✓ Visual aids
- ✓ Time of day
- ✓ Clothes

Routine
1) On your own
2) Sympathetic ears
3) Tough questions & heckles
Time yourself and stop 24 hours in advance

Specifics
- ✓ Intro and Outro
- ✓ Slower than conversation
- ✓ Emphasis in the right places **Ch 8**
- ✓ Familiar with equipment
- ✓ Handling of visual aids

Questions – 4-way preparation
1) Obvious
2) Difficult
3) FAQs – when no one asks
4) News-related

Prompt aids
- ✓ Small & stiff with 'map' to get you back on track
- ✓ Presenter Tools for PowerPoint

Plan for problems

Starbucks Test

Top 10 Tips for Delivery

1. Set up **technical equipment first** and rearrange furniture to suit yourself.

2. Do a **voice check** – whether or not you are using a microphone – to gauge the acoustics.

3. Familiarise yourself with **light switches** if you need to turn them on or off during your presentation – mark them with a spot of Blu-tack.

4. A **smile** on your face **can be heard in the voice**; and **K words** force you to smile.

5. Bring **focus** back to yourself by
    a) Using the B or W key in PowerPoint (B blacks the screen, W whites it).
    b) Move forward / lean forward / lower your voice – all bring the audience closer to you.
    c) Use the Blair/Daniels Technique – *tell them* an important point is coming.

6. **Pause** whenever you have said anything especially important. Use pauses also to a) Highlight key points b) Add dramatic impact.

7. Check the **eye colours** of your audience members – this ensures you are making close eye contact.

8. **Keep looking forwards.** Avoid the strong temptation to look at your screen – it breaks eye contact and muffles your voice. Do look at the screen if you want to draw attention to a specific point displayed.

9. Avoid ending on **Questions & Answers** if you can – keep the climax in your control. Say: "Before I conclude, would you like to ask any questions?" Take a final question and then conclude with your key points and an applause cue.

10. If **no one asks a question**, pose one yourself: "I am often asked …" This fills the awkward silence, makes it easy for you and often kick-starts a flow of genuine questions.

Delivery

Arrival Routine
✓ Familiarization
✓ Voice check and warm up
✓ Lighting
✓ Layout
✓ Remove distractions

Ch 9

Ch 15
Climax
1) Signpost the ending
2) Reiterate key messages
3) Make it definite with an
   applause cue

Ch 14
Impact issues
• Distractions in the wider
  environment
• Nodding off point
• Placement of Q&A

Engagement
• Introductions
• Opening
• Voice
  ▫ Projection, variation of pitch
    and warm up
  ▫ Pauses
• Eyes
  ▫ Close eye contact
  ▫ Well held & well spread
  ▫ Check audience eye colours
• Body
  ▫ Standing or seated?
  ▫ Stillness
  ▫ Gestures

Ch 11

Ch 13
Directing attention
Control attention grabbers
• Planning of focal points
• Anticipating distractions
• Owning the space

Re-direct attention
• Movement and change
• Flagging up key points

Handling Visual Aids
• Display clear and still – SPoF
• Linger
• Clear away as planned

Graphs & Charts
• Orientate audience with axes
• Then make your point
• Milk time lines as appropriate

Special planning for presentation by
document

PowerPoint
• Keep looking forwards
• Keep clearing the screen
 – B & W buttons
• Jump to & Hyperlinks for
  flexibility   **Ch 12**
• Use your own slide changer
• Failsafe approach to multi-media

Let it support you, not drive you

ABOUT THE AUTHOR

NICK FITZHERBERT spent 20 years in PR consultancy, working in sectors including drinks, media, marketing services, public sector, industry organizations and financial services. He worked for consultancies such as Countrywide and Ludgate, as well as running his own top-100 firm SFB for seven years.

Nick's presentation and creative skills have their roots in his years as a DJ and have been honed more recently through his experiences as a member of the world's foremost magic society, The Magic Circle. Nick's interest in magic developed mid-way through his PR career. The more he learned about magic, the more convinced he became that many of its principles for directing attention, persuading and convincing could be applied to great effect in his day job.

By matching his PR and marketing experience with research of The Magic Circle's archives and additional knowledge gained through access to some of the world's top magicians, Nick identified the Rules of Magic – 20 principles that are used instinctively by the best magicians and prove equally effective in business. Based on the way the brain takes in information, the Rules are mostly simple and intuitive and they revolve around why magic works, rather than how it works.

The Rules form the backbone of training programmes that Nick provides in Presentation Skills for sales teams, marketing agencies and other business organizations. Traditional training methods are built upon with magic-based techniques to help business people direct and hold attention, as well as persuade and convince.

Nick also speaks at conferences, CPD organizations and private members' clubs. He has been seen on TV with Adrian Chiles and heard on radio with Chris Evans. Other media appearances include: *Management Today*, *The Guardian*, *Business Life* and *CorpComms*.

Nick lives in London with his wife, Paula, and children, Louis and Eliza.

More information available at www.fitzherbert.co.uk.